THE BOOK

OF

FORMULA 1

TOP
TENS

ROGER SMITH

ABBREVIATIONS

Atmo	Normally aspirated 'Atmospheric' engine
BHP	Brake Horsepower
DFV	Double Four Valve, Ford Cosworth engine
DNQ	Did Not Qualify
DNS	Did Not Start
DSQ	Disqualified
F1	Formula 1
FIA	*Federation Internationale de l'Automobile*, motor sport's governing body
GP	Grand Prix
NC	Not Classified
Turbo	Forced induction 'Turbocharged' engine
% Strike Rate	GPs won as percent of GPs started

Unless otherwise stated, Schumacher refers to Michael
Schumacher and Nelson Piquet to the parent.

THE BOOK
OF
FORMULA 1
TOP
TENS

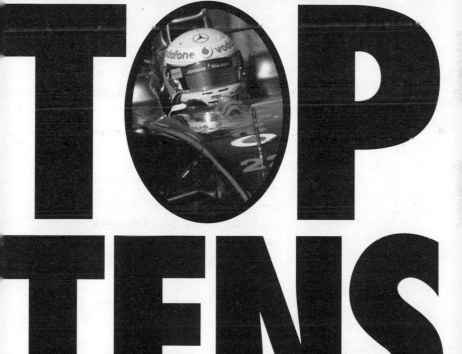

ROGER SMITH

First published in October 2008

A catalogue record for this book is available from the British Library

ISBN 978 1 84425 571 9

Library of Congress control no. 2008926358

All photographs LAT

Published by Haynes Publishing,
Sparkford, Yeovil, Somerset BA22 7JJ, UK
Tel: 01963 442030 Fax: 01963 440001
Int. tel: +44 1963 442030 Int. fax: +44 1963 440001
E-mail: sales@haynes.co.uk
Website: www.haynes.co.uk

Haynes North America Inc.
861 Lawrence Drive, Newbury Park, California 91320, USA

Printed and bound in Great Britain by
J. H. Haynes & Co. Ltd, Sparkford

CONTENTS

INTRODUCTION

On 11 March 2006, Formula 1 gave new meaning to Top Ten. It was the very first time a new knock-out qualifying format would be used to determine grid order. Qualifying would now be held in three parts, with the final Q3 session becoming a Top Ten shoot-out!

Maybe *The Book of Formula 1 Top Tens* will attach further resonance to the number ten, which until the emergence of Q3 had enjoyed a primary association with F1 of ten points for a win! As it was, on that very same Grand Prix weekend in March 2006, another F1 ten actually vanished. The banshee shriek of the ubiquitous 3-litre V10 engine at close on 20,000rpm was gone, replaced by the deeper, more moderated pitch of the 2.4-litre V8, capped at a 'mere' 19,000 revs!

This book is more unconstrained V10 than restricted V8. It provides an insightful portrayal of Grand Prix racing from 1950 to the present day in a handy pick-up-put-down 'sound-bite' format. When grabbed by the need to indulge in a little Formula 1 fever, just flick through the pages and you'll soon be hunkered down in your own virtual cockpit, savouring the sights, smells and sounds of the greatest sport on the planet.

The first Formula 1 Grand Prix counting towards the Drivers' World Championship took place in May 1950. This is the magnificent period of Grand Prix history to be enjoyed in these pages, the almost 800 Grands Prix raced since then until the present day. Between 1950 and 1960, the famous Indianapolis 500 mile race formed part of the Championship, although the cars did not actually comply with F1 regulations. For the purposes of this book, those 11 anachronistic races have been excluded throughout.

'Won't Michael Schumacher top most of the rankings?' Prior to publication, this became the most frequent question. To save checking, the answer is 11, leaving a further 73 Top Tens to the rest of the F1 fraternity! This book is about Formula 1, not any individual car, driver or race track. In fact, the 84 Top Tens are populated by almost 200 drivers as well as around 50 great cars and some 50 glorious circuits. These pages are not only testimony to the greats but equally to the also-rans. They may be seen to merely make up the numbers, but without them the good can never aspire to greatness.

Top Tens are exactly that, so what happens when two or more entries achieve the same mark or 'score'? In such circumstances, that time honoured methodology used in F1 qualifying has been adopted – chronological order. That is to say, the first to achieve a certain mark has precedence over any that subsequently match it. However, for the sake of curiosity and completeness, all such chronological exclusions provide a footnote to the relevant Top Ten table.

Finally, publication deadlines have meant that this book is spot-on up to and including the Italian GP, 14th of the gripping 18-round battle for the 2008 World Championship.

Chapter

CHAMPIONS &
CHAMPIONSHIPS

Long before it became today's TV-fuelled sporting colossus,
watched by some 600 million viewers worldwide, Grand Prix
motor racing has widely been regarded as the pinnacle of motor
sport. The ingredients essential for its massive success are sublime
drivers, great cars, glorious circuits .... and the FIA Formula 1
World Championship. The championship is the glue which binds
together this global series of races – some excitement-packed,
others not – but, with every twist and turn in the points table,
each race makes its special contribution to the compulsive World
Championship story. The drivers' championship began almost 60
years ago in 1950. Here are the highlights:

MOST WORLD CHAMPIONSHIPS

Over the 58 full seasons since the FIA Formula 1 World Championship for drivers began, Kimi Räikkönen was only the 29th driver to be crowned. The reason for this, apparent from this first Top Ten, is the high incidence of multiple champions. Just 14 champions have won a staggering 43 titles between them. Alberto Ascari was the first back-to-back champion, but the legendary Juan Manuel Fangio, *the Maestro,* established a seemingly unbeatable early benchmark of five titles. *Le Professeur,* Alain Prost, came close, but not until the fourth of Schumacher's five-titles-in-a-row with Ferrari, itself an unprecedented achievement, did Fangio's 45-year record eventually fall. There are three in this distinguished Top Ten – Alberto Ascari, Jim Clark, and Ayrton Senna – who might well have accomplished much more, but each perished at the wheel in an unforgiving sport where, even today, disaster still stalks. Their curtailed careers left three unfulfilled track rivalries which might well have significantly reshaped this list: Ascari vs. Fangio; Clark vs. Stewart, and Senna vs. Schumacher. Fernando Alonso is the latest double World Champion, an achievement Kimi Räikkönen may still be keen to emulate. But Lewis Hamilton probably has other ideas!

1. **MICHAEL SCHUMACHER**
1994, 1995 (Benetton); 2000, 2001, 2002, 2003, 2004 (Ferrari)
7

2. **JUAN MANUEL FANGIO**
1951 (Alfa Romeo); 1954 (Maserati & Mercedes-Benz);
1955 (Mercedes-Benz); 1956 (Ferrari); 1957 (Maserati)
5

3. **ALAIN PROST**
1985, 1986, 1989 (McLaren); 1993 (Williams)
4

4. **JACK BRABHAM**
1959, 1960 (Cooper); 1966 (Brabham)
3

5. **JACKIE STEWART**
1969 (Matra [Tyrrell]); 1971, 1973 (Tyrrell)
3

6. **NIKI LAUDA**
1975, 1977 (Ferrari); 1984 (McLaren)
3

7. **NELSON PIQUET**
1981, 1983 (Brabham); 1987 (Williams)
3

8. **AYRTON SENNA**
1988, 1990, 1991 (McLaren)
3

9. **ALBERTO ASCARI**
1952, 1953 (Ferrari)
2

10. **JIM CLARK**
1963, 1965 (Lotus)
2

Also double World Champions were GRAHAM HILL 1962 (BRM); 1968 (Lotus); EMERSON FITTIPALDI 1972 (Lotus);
1974 (McLaren); MIKA HÄKKINEN 1998, 1999 (McLaren); FERNANDO ALONSO 2005, 2006 (Renault).

LONGEST WAITS FOR CHAMPIONSHIP CROWN

Until his late-season surge snatched the title from Lewis Hamilton's grasp, it seemed after 120 races that it was not going to happen for Kimi Räikkönen, the reigning World Champion taking second spot in this Top Ten list of tenacity. But the daddy of them all, Nigel Mansell, took 13 seasons and 176 races before he landed his one-and-only title. Jenson Button and others can take heed – and encouragement! The tale of Mansell's championship is one of self-belief, determination, and stamina, and really he could have been a four-time World Champion (1986-87, and 1991-92). When such a great name as Alain Prost – destined ultimately to win four titles – ranks fifth on the list, it illustrates just how easy it is for opportunities to slip away. It also shows how important it is for all the ingredients making up a championship season to come together and remain intact until the job is done: a lesson learnt the hard way by Lewis Hamilton – his lost championship opportunity in 2007 one, it is hoped, he will not live to regret. It confirms just how difficult a task it is to win the championship just once, let alone numerous times.

		RACES
1.	**NIGEL MANSELL** 1992 (Williams) 13th active season	**176**
2.	**KIMI RÄIKKÖNEN** 2007 (Ferrari) 7th active season	**121**
3.	**MIKA HÄKKINEN** 1998 (McLaren) 8th active season	**112**
4.	**JODY SCHECKTER** 1979 (Ferrari) 7th active season	**97**
5.	**ALAIN PROST** 1985 (McLaren) 6th active season	**87**
6.	**MARIO ANDRETTI** 1978 (Lotus) 10th active season	**80**
7.	**ALAN JONES** 1980 (Williams) 6th active season	**80**
8.	**AYRTON SENNA** 1988 (McLaren) 5th active season	**77**
9.	**DAMON HILL** 1996 (Williams) 5th active season	**67**
10.	**FERNANDO ALONSO** 2005 (Renault) 5th active season	**67**

1.3

MOST EXCITING CHAMPIONSHIPS

The consistent dynamic which heightened the tension and excitement within this Top Ten is that each championship was decided at the season finale. And in four of these seasons, three drivers entered that final race in contention for championship honours; not least the intense and thrilling championships placed second and third, those epics of 1986 and 2007. But 1976 stands at number one, a championship battle so compelling that it is often parodied as 'The greatest story ever told'. What special ingredient made it so – Hunt versus Lauda? Ford versus Ferrari? McLaren versus Maranello? – it contained every facet which transforms a good script into great theatre: the unexpected, disqualifications, reinstatements, intrigue, dirty tricks, last rites, courage, bravery, all culminating in a showdown at the Fuji finale. These 100 minutes of racing were in themselves a microcosm of all the emotional turmoil that had gone before, finally to be resolved between two most worthy contenders by just a single point! Rounding out this list are two seasons which condone the McLaren and condemn the (latter-day) Ferrari approach to racing: in those wonderful intra-team championship battles of 1984 and 1988, there were no team orders!

1. **JAMES HUNT**
(McLaren) 69 championship points beat
Niki Lauda (Ferrari) 68 championship points
1976

2. **ALAIN PROST**
(McLaren) 72 championship points beat
Nigel Mansell (Williams) 70 championship points
1986

3. **KIMI RÄIKKÖNEN**
(Ferrari) 120 championship points beat
Lewis Hamilton (McLaren) 119 championship points
2007

4. **MIKE HAWTHORN**
(Ferrari) 42 championship points beat
Stirling Moss (Vanwall) 41 championship points
1958

5. **GRAHAM HILL**
(BRM) 42 championship points beat
Jim Clark (Lotus) 30 championship points
1962

6. **MICHAEL SCHUMACHER**
(Benetton) 92 championship points beat
Damon Hill (Williams) 91 championship points
1994

7. **JOHN SURTEES**
(Ferrari) 40 championship points beat
Graham Hill (BRM) 39 championship points
1964

8. **GRAHAM HILL**
(Lotus) 48 championship points beat
Jackie Stewart (Matra [Tyrrell]) 36 championship points
1968

9. **NIKI LAUDA**
(McLaren) 72 championship points beat
Alain Prost (McLaren) 71.5 championship points
1984

10. **AYRTON SENNA**
(McLaren) 90 championship points beat
Alain Prost (McLaren) 87 championship points
1988

MOST DOMINANT CHAMPIONSHIP SEASONS

'Most *dominant* championship season' rarely coincides with 'Most *exciting* championship season'. Certainly Michael Schumacher's succession of dominant championships with Ferrari seldom produced either thrilling racing or an exciting championship battle. In 2004 he raised his own 2002 record to a staggering 13 victories in a season! But such dominance is not a new phenomenon. As early as 1952 Alberto Ascari established a benchmark of six victories, again for Ferrari, which Jim Clark raised to seven in 1963. Ayrton Senna took it to eight in 1988, and Nigel Mansell posted nine wins in his triumphant 1992 season. Although such high scores suggest total dominance by one driver, this list hides certain exceptions, most evidently 1988, when Senna won his eight races against Prost's seven. Another consideration is strike rate, the number of wins achieved from the number of races started. Schumacher won his 13 in 2004 from 18 starts (72 per cent strike rate) whereas Ascari's ostensibly modest six in 1952 came from only seven race starts, an extraordinary 86 per cent which, for the sake of future championship excitement, it is hoped will stand for ever!

1. **MICHAEL SCHUMACHER** **13**
2004 (Ferrari) 13 victories from 18 races, 72 per cent strike rate

2. **MICHAEL SCHUMACHER** **11**
2002 (Ferrari) 11 victories from 17 races, 65 per cent strike rate

3. **NIGEL MANSELL** **9**
1992 (Williams) 9 victories from 16 races, 56 per cent strike rate

4. **MICHAEL SCHUMACHER** **9**
1995 (Benetton) 9 victories from 17 races, 53 per cent strike rate

5. **MICHAEL SCHUMACHER** **9**
2000 (Ferrari) 9 victories from 17 races, 53 per cent strike rate

6. **MICHAEL SCHUMACHER** **9**
2001 (Ferrari) 9 victories from 17 races, 53 per cent strike rate

7. **AYRTON SENNA** **8**
1988 (McLaren) 8 victories from 16 races, 50 per cent strike rate

8. **MICHAEL SCHUMACHER** **8**
1994 (Benetton) 8 victories from 16 races, 50 per cent strike rate

9. **DAMON HILL** **8**
1996 (Williams) 8 victories from 16 races, 50 per cent strike rate

10. **MIKA HÄKKINEN** **8**
1998 (McLaren) 8 victories from 16 races, 50 per cent strike rate

1.5

MOST CAREER CHAMPIONSHIP POINTS

The FIA Formula 1 World Championship is based on a system of points accumulated over a series of races. Ten points are currently awarded for first place, down to one for eighth, the driver with the highest total at season-end being crowned champion. Championship points are a highly valued commodity by Grand Prix drivers and teams alike. A drivers' status and market value will be influenced by his points standing in the championship table, whereas for a team, position not only determines their share of the commercial rights from television and other sources, but even their slot in the pit-lane. In Formula 1, points truly do mean prizes! Michael Schumacher's phenomenal points score results from a lengthy career at or near the top of his sport, including an unprecedented record of ten-point-scoring race victories. This Top Ten features only two non-World Champions – veterans Coulthard and Barrichello – neither of whom are prolific winners but still ply their trade because of their sustained points-scoring ability, as confirmed by their strong points-per-race average. Speaking of which, although his absolute points tally doesn't signify a Top Ten placing, on a like-for-like basis, Juan Manuel Fangio's points-per-race average would outscore even Schumacher!

1. **MICHAEL SCHUMACHER**
5.5 points-per-race average from 249 race starts — **1,369**

2. **ALAIN PROST**
4.0 points-per-race average from 199 race starts — **798.5**

3. **AYRTON SENNA**
3.8 points-per-race average from 161 race starts — **614**

4. **DAVID COULTHARD**
2.2 points-per-race average from 242 race starts — **533**

5. **RUBENS BARRICHELLO**
2.0 points-per-race average from 264 race starts — **530**

6. **FERNANDO ALONSO**
4.4 points-per-race average from 118 race starts — **518**

7. **KIMI RÄIKKÖNEN**
3.8 points-per-race average from 135 race starts — **513**

8. **NELSON PIQUET**
2.4 points-per-race average from 204 race starts — **485.5**

9. **NIGEL MANSELL**
2.6 points-per-race average from 187 race starts — **482**

10. **NIKI LAUDA**
2.5 points-per-race average from 171 race starts — **420.5**

NARROWEST POINTS MARGIN TO WIN A CHAMPIONSHIP

A close championship finish usually means an exciting finish, so there is inevitably some correlation between this Top Ten and 1.3. That said, it should not come as too much of a surprise that numerous championships have been resolved by a mere handful of points. The reason is that over the years the FIA have used various devices within the championship points scoring system to deliver exactly that end-result. Currently it is achieved by a narrow gap between the points awarded for each place, whereby, although Kimi Räikkönen won two more race victories than Lewis Hamilton, he only won the 2007 championship by a single point. Alain Prost, the driver to uniquely lose a title by one-half-of-one-point, would have to accept the maxim that 'Those who live by the sword, die by the sword'. He was a championship points beneficiary (twice) as well as its victim! In this Top Ten of close championship finishes, only one did not go down-to-the-wire. In 1961, due to the tragedy at Monza which befell Wolfgang von Trips, Enzo Ferrari withdrew his cars from the final round as a mark of respect.

1.

NIKI LAUDA
1984 (McLaren) 72 championship points beat
Alain Prost (McLaren) 71.5 championship points

0.5

2.

MIKE HAWTHORN
1958 (Ferrari) 42 championship points beat
Stirling Moss (Vanwall) 41 championship points

1

3.

PHIL HILL
1961 (Ferrari) 34 championship points beat
Wolfgang von Trips (Ferrari) 33 championship points

1

4.

JOHN SURTEES
1964 (Ferrari) 40 championship points beat
Graham Hill (BRM) 39 championship points

1

5.

JAMES HUNT
1976 (McLaren) 69 championship points beat
Niki Lauda (Ferrari) 68 championship points

1

6.

NELSON PIQUET
1981 (Brabham) 50 championship points beat
Carlos Reutemann (Williams) 49 championship points

1

7.

MICHAEL SCHUMACHER
1994 (Benetton) 92 championship points beat
Damon Hill (Williams) 91 championship points

1

8.

KIMI RÄIKKÖNEN
2007 (Ferrari) 120 championship points beat
Lewis Hamilton (McLaren) 119 championship points

1

9.

NELSON PIQUET
1983 (Brabham) 59 championship points beat
Alain Prost (Renault) 57 championship points

2

10.

ALAIN PROST
1986 (McLaren) 72 championship points beat
Nigel Mansell (Williams) 70 championship points

2

FEWEST VICTORIES TO WIN A CHAMPIONSHIP

However well conceived, any points-based system can occasionally produce eccentricities, and the drivers' World Championship has had its share. Although down-to-the-wire championships and runaway championships form the two extremes, there is a third and perhaps more controversial category which is sometimes paradoxically labelled 'beaten champions'. This refers to the 11 occasions – seven of which find their way into this Top Ten – when a rival has won more races than the champion in their championship year. As winning is everything in Formula 1, it is somewhat incongruous that the championship points system rewards losers so generously. As already explained, this keeps the title battle alive for longer, but can result in the possibility of a less than worthy champion.

Thankfully, a Formula 1 World Champion has never been crowned having not won a race at all, but on two occasions just one victory sufficed. In 1958 Mike Hawthorn won just once from his ten race starts (10 per cent strike rate) and in 1982 Keke Rosberg's sole victory came from 15 (7 per cent).

1. **MIKE HAWTHORN**
1958 (Ferrari) 1 victory from 10 races, 10 per cent strike rate
1

2. **KEKE ROSBERG**
1982 (Williams) 1 victory from 16 races, 7 per cent strike rate
1

3. **JACK BRABHAM**
1959 (Cooper) 2 victories from 8 races, 25 per cent strike rate
2

4. **PHIL HILL**
1961 (Ferrari) 2 victories from 8 races, 25 per cent strike rate
2

5. **JOHN SURTEES**
1964 (Ferrari) 2 victories from 10 races, 20 per cent strike rate
2

6. **DENNY HULME**
1967 (Brabham) 2 victories from 11 races, 18 per cent strike rate
2

7. **EMERSON FITTIPALDI**
1974 (McLaren) 3 victories from 15 races, 20 per cent strike rate
3

8. **NIKI LAUDA**
1977 (Ferrari) 3 victories from 17 races, 18 per cent strike rate
3

9. **JODY SCHECKTER**
1979 (Ferrari) 3 victories from 15 races, 20 per cent strike rate
3

10. **NELSON PIQUET**
1987 (Williams) 3 victories from 16 races, 19 per cent strike rate
3

MOST RACE WINS WITHOUT A CHAMPIONSHIP

This Top Ten might well be entitled 'the nearly men'. It includes six of the 23 drivers who never became World Champion but finished in the runner-up spot. Coming home second in any championship must be galling, not least, as in some of these cases, when it happens in the wake of a teammate's championship conquest driving 'equal' equipment. The most mortifying example must be the subservient role Rubens Barrichello was contractually obliged to play to Michael Schumacher at Ferrari, being required to move over even on those rare occasions when he held sway. Stirling Moss played the number-two role to Fangio when they were teamed together at Mercedes-Benz in 1955. This was the first of an unprecedented four successive finishes as runner-up, Moss gaining the dubious accolade of the greatest driver never to win the World Championship. The one that really got away was 1958 when, through a mixture of altruism and confused pit signals at Oporto, Stirling ultimately lost the championship by a single point. Of the currently active drivers, Felipe Massa is fighting hard to avoid being one of 'the nearly men'. With Ferrari he will never get a better chance.

1. **STIRLING MOSS**
Championship runner-up 1955 (to Fangio), 1956 (to Fangio), 1957 (to Fangio) and 1958 (to Hawthorn)

16

2. **DAVID COULTHARD**
Championship runner-up 2001 (to M. Schumacher)

13

3. **CARLOS REUTEMANN**
Championship runner-up 1981 (to N. Piquet)

12

4. **RONNIE PETERSON**
Championship runner-up 1971 (to Stewart) and 1978 (to Mario Andretti)

10

5. **GERHARD BERGER**
Best championship placing, 3rd 1988, 1990 and 1994

10

6. **FELIPE MASSA**
Best championship placing, 3rd 2006

10

7. **RUBENS BARRICHELLO**
Championship runner-up 2002 (to M. Schumacher) and 2004 (to M. Schumacher)

9

8. **JACKY ICKX**
Championship runner-up 1969 (to Stewart) and 1970 (to Rindt)

8

9. **LEWIS HAMILTON**
Championship runner-up 2007 (to K. Räikkönen)

8

10. **RENE ARNOUX**
Best championship placing, 3rd 1983

7

JUAN PABLO MONTOYA also won 7 races without a championship.

MOST GRANDS PRIX BY COUNTRY

Imbued with extreme passion for their beloved Scuderia Ferrari, it seems fitting that the *Tifosi*, as Italian F1 fans are known, have been granted championship status to more Grand Prix races than any other country. Italy's 85 Grands Prix in the 59th year of the World Championships are due to a second race at the Imola circuit on behalf of the principality of San Marino – sadly no longer on the calendar. Numerous devices have been found by circuit promoters to run a second World Championship F1 race in their country. Perhaps the most bizarre examples have been the Luxembourg GP run in Germany (Nürburgring 1997 and 1998) and the Swiss GP in France (Dijon-Prénois 1982), particularly as motor sport was banned in Switzerland after the 1955 Le Mans disaster! But the most popular ploy was to run the European Grand Prix as a separate entity, an arrangement Germany benefited from during the great Schumacher years when the *Fatherland* could readily support a second race each year. Only one country has staged more than two Grands Prix in a single season. In 1982 three championship races were held in the USA: Long Beach, Detroit, and Las Vegas. Today there's not even one!

1. ITALY **86**
Italian GP: Monza 58; Imola 1. Pescara GP: 1. San Marino GP: Imola 26

2. GERMANY **69**
German GP: Hockenheim 31; Nürburgring 26; The AVUS 1.
European GP: Nürburgring 9. Luxembourg GP: Nürburgring 2

3. GREAT BRITAIN **62**
British GP: Silverstone 42; Brands Hatch 12; Aintree 5.
European GP: Brands Hatch 2; Donington 1

4. FRANCE **59**
French GP: Magny-Cours 18; Paul Ricard 14; Reims 11; Rouen 5; Dijon 5;
Clermont Ferrand 4; Bugatti au Mans 1. Swiss GP: Dijon 1

5. MONACO **55**
Monaco GP: Monte-Carlo 55

6. BELGIUM **53**
Belgian GP: Spa-Francorchamps 41; Zolder 10: Nivelles 2

7. UNITED STATES **52**
US GP: Watkins Glen 20; Indianapolis 9; Phoenix 3; Sebring 1; Riverside 1.
US GP (West): Long Beach 8. Caesars Palace GP: Las Vegas 2.
Detroit: 7. Dallas GP: 1

8. SPAIN **41**
Spanish GP: Catalunya 18; Jarama 9; Jerez 5; Montjuïc 4; Pedralbes 2
European GP: Jerez 2; Valencia 1

9. CANADA **40**
Canadian GP: Montreal 30; Mosport Park 8; Saint-Jovite 2

10. BRAZIL **34**
Brazilian GP: Interlagos 25; Rio 10

YOUNGEST WORLD CHAMPIONS

If rookie Lewis Hamilton had triumphed in 2007 he would have established a new record as the youngest World Champion. And he still can, although 2008 is his second and last chance. This Top Ten operates on at least two levels. It ranks by age the ten youngest champions, but only three of those listed – just as Hamilton still might – actually established a new youthful benchmark. The first under-30 title-holder was 1958 champion Mike Hawthorn. The three who preceded him were appreciably older, as were the trio who followed. So it was not until 1963 that Jim Clark again lowered the record, and a further nine years were to go by until an extraordinary new landmark was reached. In 1972, Emerson Fittipaldi not only decimated the record by a further two years, but it was to stand unbeaten for an astonishing 33 years! Season after season, Formula 1 greats came and went, and, although Michael Schumacher came close, no one took their first title at a younger age. Not until a young Spaniard, who then also held the accolade as the youngest Grand Prix race winner, beat Kimi Räikkönen to the title in 2005.

1.	**FERNANDO ALONSO*** 2005 (Renault) beat Kimi Räikkönen (McLaren), establishing a new benchmark	**24y** **1m 27d**
2.	**EMERSON FITTIPALDI** 1972 (Lotus) beat Jackie Stewart (Tyrrell), establishing a new benchmark	**25y** **8m 29d**
3.	**MICHAEL SCHUMACHER** 1994 (Ferrari) beat Damon Hill (Williams)	**25y** **10m 10d**
4.	**NIKI LAUDA** 1975 (Ferrari) beat Emerson Fittipaldi (McLaren)	**26y** **6m 16d**
5.	**JACQUES VILLENEUVE** 1997 (Williams) beat Heinz-Harald Frentzen (Williams) following M. Schumacher's disqualification	**26y** **6m 17d**
6.	**JIM CLARK** 1963 (Lotus) beat Graham Hill (BRM), establishing a new benchmark	**27y** **6m 4d**
7.	**KIMI RÄIKKÖNEN** 2007 (Ferrari) beat Lewis Hamilton (McLaren)	**28y** **0m 4d**
8.	**JOCHEN RINDT** 1970 (Lotus) beat Jacky Ickx (Ferrari)	**28y** **4m 18d**
9.	**AYRTON SENNA** 1988 (McLaren) beat Alain Prost (McLaren)	**28y** **7m 9d**
10.	**JAMES HUNT** 1976 (McLaren) beat Niki Lauda (Ferrari)	**29y** **1m 25d**

*FERNANDO ALONSO is also the youngest double World Champion.

Chapter

WINNERS AND DOMINATORS

Grand Prix racing is all about winning. As Gilles Villeneuve put it, 'Finishing second means you are the first person to lose'! From 1950 to date, 788 races have been won from a pool of 626 drivers, making 17,787 Grand Prix starts. And yet a mere 91 have actually taken the chequered flag. This remarkable statistic signifies that as well as race winners in F1 there are also dominators, a handful of racing drivers who win, win, and win again. In fact, the Top Ten of those 91 Grand Prix race winners – just ten drivers – account for nearly half of all the 788 race victories. Chapter 2 opens with a close look at these Top Ten 'serial winners'.

MOST CAREER RACE VICTORIES

Fangio's 1957 victory at the Nürburgring brought his final aggregate of race wins to a seemingly untouchable 24, well ahead of the late lamented Alberto Ascari's record tally at his death of 13. Jim Clark's spate of 1960s successes made Fangio's record seem suddenly vulnerable, and on 1 January 1968 he duly exceeded it – only to die at the wheel barely 100 days later. It was to be another Scot, John Young (Jackie) Stewart, who gave the record a further nudge when he completed his career in 1973 with 27 victories to his name. Now another 14 years would pass before Frenchman Alain Prost surpassed Stewart, but when he departed the driver scene at the close of 1993, he and two others had rewritten the record books: Prost 51; Senna 41; Mansell 30 (he was to win once more). The expectation was that, with Prost's retirement, Senna would go on to surpass his phenomenal total, but events on 1 May 1994 meant this scenario was not to be. Instead, Michael Schumacher not only surpassed Prost in 2003, he transformed the record to 91 victories, virtually the same as Prost and Senna combined. Now that's untouchable – isn't it?

1. **MICHAEL SCHUMACHER**
Benetton 19 (1991-95); Ferrari 72 (1996-2006)
91

2. **ALAIN PROST**
Renault 9 (1981-83); McLaren 30 (1980 and 1984-89);
Ferrari 5 (1990-91); Williams 7 (1993)
51

3. **AYRTON SENNA**
Lotus 6 (1985-87); McLaren 35 (1988-1993)
41

4. **NIGEL MANSELL**
Williams 28 (1985-88, 1991-92 and 1994); Ferrari 3 (1989-90)
31

5. **JACKIE STEWART**
BRM 2 (1965-67); Tyrrell Matra 9 (1968-69); Tyrrell March 1 (1970);
Tyrrell 15 (1970-73)
27

6. **JIM CLARK**
Lotus 25 (1960-68)
25

7. **NIKI LAUDA**
Ferrari 15 (1974-77); Brabham 2 (1978-79); McLaren 8 (1982-85)
25

8. **JUAN MANUEL FANGIO**
Alfa Romeo 6 (1950-51); Maserati 7 (1953-54 and 1957); Mercedes-
Benz 8 (1954-55); Ferrari 3 (1956)
24

9. **NELSON PIQUET**
Brabham 13 (1978-85); Williams 7 (1986-87); Benetton 3 (1990-91)
23

10. **DAMON HILL**
Williams 21 (1993-96); Jordan 1 (1998-99)
22

HIGHEST STRIKE RATE*

Michael Schumacher's staggering 91 race victories may stand forever – but absolutes provide just one measure. His winning haul was generated over an inordinately long career in which he took part in more races than any other driver bar two. So, to achieve his victory record, Schumacher also competed in 158 races which he failed to win. To place a win record into context and relate it to another, it is generally accepted that the number of starts is applied to create a ratio normally referred to as 'strike rate'. Thus, wins as a percentage of starts equals per cent strike rate. Juan Manuel Fangio heads this Top Ten with a strike rate of almost one win in every two starts (47 per cent). To place it in perspective, Michael Schumacher would have needed to add a further 26 successive Grand Prix victories to his vast tally in order to match Fangio's record! Surely the most unexpected name to appear on this list (and the preceding one) is Damon Hill. Having won regularly over the years against more vaunted teammates and rivals, these figures prove Hill to be one of the most underrated of winners.

1. **JUAN MANUEL FANGIO**
24 race victories (2 shared) from 51 Grand Prix starts
47

2. **ALBERTO ASCARI**
13 race victories from 31 Grand Prix starts
42

3. **MICHAEL SCHUMACHER**
91 race victories from 249 Grand Prix starts
37

4. **JIM CLARK**
25 race victories from 72 Grand Prix starts
35

5. **JACKIE STEWART**
27 race victories from 99 Grand Prix starts
27

6. **ALAIN PROST**
51 race victories from 199 Grand Prix starts
26

7. **AYRTON SENNA**
41 race victories from 161 Grand Prix starts
25

8. **STIRLING MOSS**
16 race victories (1 shared) from 66 Grand Prix starts
24

9. **DAMON HILL**
22 race victories from 115 Grand Prix starts
19

10. **NIGEL MANSELL**
31 race victories from 187 Grand Prix starts
17

*Drivers with 10 or more race victories

FEWEST RACES TO FIRST VICTORY

In 2007 Lewis Hamilton hit the headlines by winning his sixth ever Grand Prix. Although it was a terrific achievement, some of his predecessors had done even better. Realistically, Farina and Fangio, winners of the very first two Formula 1 Grands Prix in 1950, should be discounted from this list, leaving Italian Giancarlo Baghetti as the only driver ever to win on debut since the World Championship began. His story is quite extraordinary in that earlier that same season he won his two very first Formula 1 races – admittedly non-Championship events – which made this dream Championship win at Reims his third Formula 1 victory in as many races. On each occasion he drove a Ferrari 156, very much the car of the moment in 1961, but on that triumphant day in France, with his three Ferrari teammates all sidelined, it was he who had been left to uphold the honours of the Prancing Horse. Baghetti was never to win again, or even mount the podium. A career which began with such glitter and promise faded into obscurity, but his name will forever be part of F1 folklore – the driver who won on debut.

1. **NINO FARINA**
Alfa Romeo – 1950 British GP:
Winner of the inaugural World Championship race
1

2. **GIANCARLO BAGHETTI**
Ferrari – 1961 French GP: The only driver to win on debut
1

3. **JUAN MANUEL FANGIO**
Alfa Romeo – 1950 Monaco GP: Winner of Round 2, the first Monaco GP
2

4. **TONY BROOKS**
Vanwall – 1957 British GP: Shared the first win for a British car
with Moss
3

5. **LUDOVICO SCARFIOTTI**
Ferrari – 1966 Italian GP: With Ascari, the only Italian-Ferrari-Monza
winners
4

6. **EMERSON FITTIPALDI**
Lotus – 1970 US GP: Helped Rindt to posthumous championship
4

7. **JACQUES VILLENEUVE**
Williams – 1996 European GP: Very nearly the second 'on debut' winner
4

8. **FROILAN GONZALEZ**
Ferrari – 1951 British GP: Gave Ferrari their first
World Championship victory
5

9. **CLAY REGAZZONI**
Ferrari – 1970 Italian GP: The Swiss-Italian was Ferrari-mounted at
Monza
5

10. **LEWIS HAMILTON**
McLaren – 2007 Canadian GP: What took him so long?
6

2.4

MOST RACES TO FIRST VICTORY

Mounting the top step of the Formula 1 podium marks a feat so challenging, so exceptional, that it may be equated to winning an Olympic Gold Medal. Since the inception of the World Championship close to 60 years ago, it has been accomplished by a mere 89 drivers. For a fortunate few it happens quickly (see 2.3), but when that first win comes after many years of trying, it is enough to stir the emotions of those with even the most resolute self belief. The media-led pressure placed on Jenson Button before his 2006 victory is still a recent memory. Some late developers go on to win again whereas others, such as Alesi, Trulli and maybe Button, have to be content with their singleton triumph. But for two in this Top Ten, Häkkinen and Mansell, that first sweet taste of victory led on to much greater things. Mansell's story is chronicled elsewhere (see 1.2), but Hakkinen's is no less remarkable. Following a life threatening accident in 1993, Mika took almost 100 races to belatedly discover the secret of winning. On average over the remaining 65 races of his career, he won virtually every third race, a formidable strike-rate which delivered back-to-back Championships (1998–99).

1.	**RUBENS BARRICHELLO** 2000 German GP: At last, in his eighth season and eleventh race with Ferrari. No wonder the tears flowed.	**124**
2.	**JARNO TRULLI** 2004 Monaco GP: If it's going to be just the one victory, a nice one to tell the grandchildren.	**117**
3.	**JENSON BUTTON** 2006 Hungarian GP: Is it to be just the one, or will new regulations make it all come right in the end?	**113**
4.	**GIANCARLO FISICHELLA** 2003 Brazilian GP: Bizarrely, awarded initially to Räikkönen, Fisi's first victory was Jordan's last hurrah.	**110**
5.	**MIKA HÄKKINEN** 1997 European GP: A gifted first victory unleashed an exceptional championship career.	**96**
6.	**THIERRY BOUTSEN** 1989 Canadian GP: A pioneer and deserving beneficiary of the Williams-Renault phenomenon.	**95**
7.	**JEAN ALESI** 1995 Canadian GP: His one and only victory came in his fifth and final season with his beloved Ferrari.	**91**
8.	**EDDIE IRVINE** 1999 Australian GP: Riding shotgun to Schumacher at Ferrari did have its compensations…eventually.	**81**
9.	**NIGEL MANSELL** 1985 European GP: This late developer became the fourth most prolific all-time winner with 31 victories.	**72**
10.	**JOHNNY HERBERT** 1995 British GP: For your breakthrough victory, where better than your home Grand Prix at Silverstone.	**71**

MOST SUCCESSIVE GP VICTORIES

Despite Michael Schumacher's utter dominance of the opening to the new millennium, he failed to separate Alberto Ascari from a record set more than 50 years before. Ascari's dominance of 1952/53 is legendary: 14 starts; 11 wins, 9 in succession. However, this remarkable record requires qualification. It excludes the Indianapolis 500-mile race, then counting towards the drivers' title. For the purposes of World Championship records, the omission of this uniquely North American race is not unusual. But conversely, Ascari and Ferrari made an attempt to win at the Brickyard in 1952, the only significant F1 team/driver so to do while the Indy 500 remained officially part of the championship. For this reason, the accepted norm is less obvious. The facts are that, after seven successive wins, Ascari's nine-in-a-row record was punctuated by an Indy 500 race. But it was one in which he, Ferrari, or any other F1 team for that matter did not participate, and on which premise his successive-nine-wins record is ratified. In any case, Michael Schumacher came mighty close to destroying Ascari's long-standing record. In 2004, apart from a rare Monaco mistake, he would have won a mere 13 Grands Prix in succession (see table).

1. **ALBERTO ASCARI**
Ferrari. Between 1952 Belgian GP and 1953 Belgian GP
9

2. **MICHAEL SCHUMACHER**
Ferrari. Between 2004 European GP and 2004 Hungarian GP
7

3. **MICHAEL SCHUMACHER**
Ferrari. Between 2000 Italian GP and 2001 Malaysian GP
6

4. **JACK BRABHAM**
Cooper. Between 1960 Dutch GP and 1960 Portuguese GP
5

5. **JIM CLARK**
Lotus. Between 1965 Belgian GP and 1965 German GP
5

6. **NIGEL MANSELL**
Williams. Between 1992 South African GP and 1992 San Marino GP
5

7. **MICHAEL SCHUMACHER**
Ferrari. Between 2004 Australian GP and 2004 Spanish GP
5

8. **JUAN MANUEL FANGIO**
Maserati & Mercedes-Benz. Between 1953 Italian GP and 1954 French GP
4

9. **JIM CLARK**
Lotus. Between 1963 Belgian GP and 1963 British GP
4

10. **JACK BRABHAM**
Brabham. Between 1966 French GP and 1966 German GP
4

Also with four successive race victories were JOCHEN RINDT 1970; AYRTON SENNA 1988 & 1991; ALAIN PROST 1993; MICHAEL SCHUMACHER 1994 & 2002; DAMON HILL 1995-96; FERNANDO ALONSO 2006.

YOUNGEST GRAND PRIX WINNERS

First to congratulate Sebastian Vettel on his historic 2008 Monza victory was Fernando Alonso. The gesture was special because the young German, driving for Fernando's erstwhile team Minardi (now Toro Rosso), had just separated him from a clutch of his impressive array of 'youngest' titles. By end-2005 Alonso claimed most of the performance-led accolades as youngest race-winner, podium-winner, pole-sitter, fastest-lap-holder and World Champion. Another young German, Nico Rosberg, began the erosion with fastest lap on his debut at the 2006 Bahrain GP, and now, along with his Monza pole, Vettel had just snatched three more. The Spaniard's good grace reflects well on Sebastian, who is widely liked in the paddock and the press-room for his genial courtesy which, compared with Scott Speed's tenure last season, creates a very different chemistry at Toro Rosso. With ever-popular Gerhard Berger also on the podium to accept the Monza winner's trophy for a non-manufacturer-owned Ferrari-engined Scuderia, it was altogether a joyous occasion, no doubt also fulfilling certain aspirations of Red Bull's founder, Dietrich Mateschitz.

		AGE
1.	**SEBASTIAN VETTEL** Toro Rosso – 2008 Italian GP: German and Italian anthems played with renewed gusto	**21y 2m 11d**
2.	**FERNANDO ALONSO** Renault - 2003 Hungarian GP: Beat Bruce's 44-year-old record	**22y 0m 26d**
3.	**BRUCE McLAREN** Cooper – 1959 US GP: Bruce lowered Hawthorn's record by two years	**22y 3m 12d**
4.	**LEWIS HAMILTON** McLaren – 2007 Canadian GP: Youngest rookie winner	**22y 5m 13d**
5.	**KIMI RÄIKKÖNEN** McLaren – 2003 Malaysian GP: Finally, after 2002 French GP slid away	**23y 5m 6d**
6.	**ROBERT KUBICA** BMW – 2008 Canadian GP: Truly laid any ghosts from 2007	**23y 6m 1d**
7.	**JACKY ICKX** Ferrari – 1968 French GP: Maiden victory in tragic circumstances	**23y 6m 6d**
8.	**MICHAEL SCHUMACHER** Benetton – 1992 Belgian GP: The first; just 90 to go!	**23y 7m 27d**
9.	**EMERSON FITTIPALDI** Lotus – 1970 US GP: Only his fourth GP start	**23y 9m 22d**
10.	**MIKE HAWTHORN** Ferrari – 1953 French GP: Britain's first GP victor	**24y 3m 25d**

MOST WINNERS IN ONE SEASON

The number of winning drivers per season has ranged from just two (twice), to a remarkable 11 in 1982. As so often, 'tyre wars' contributed to the variety of winners, but the primary cause was that 1982 was the watershed between two radically different engine technologies. On a 'power' circuit, the up-and-coming turbocharged-engined teams could blow the Ford V8 DFV-equipped cars into the weeds, but on a 'handling' track, a nimble DFV-powered chassis, with progressive torque from its 'atmo' engine, could still be the car to have. A high proportion of street circuits in the 1982 calendar – Long Beach, Monaco, Detroit, the car park at Caesar's Palace in Las Vegas; plus even Zolder, Dijon-Prénois and Brands Hatch – gave the durable DFV a fighting chance. Ultimately, honours were about even with five teams winning seven races using the Ford DFV, and three nine races with turbos (Brabham using both). The 1982 season will always be remembered as the last hurrah for the venerable DFV, but even more so for the tragedy which befell Gilles Villeneuve.

1. **1982** Rosberg, Pironi, Watson, Prost, Lauda, Arnoux, Tambay, Alboreto, de Angelis, Patrese, Piquet — **11**

2. **1975** Lauda, Fittipaldi, Reutemann, Hunt, Regazzoni, Pace, Scheckter, Mass, Brambilla — **9**

3. **1977** Lauda, Scheckter, Andretti, Reutemann, Hunt, Jones, Nilsson, Laffite — **8**

4. **1983** Piquet, Prost, Arnoux, Tambay, Rosberg, Watson, Patrese, Alboreto — **8**

5. **1985** Prost, Alboreto, Rosberg, Senna, de Angelis, Mansell, Piquet, Lauda — **8**

6. **2003** M. Schumacher, Räikkönen, Montoya, Barrichello, R. Schumacher, Alonso, Coulthard, Fisichella — **8**

7. **1968** G. Hill, Stewart, Hulme, Ickx, McLaren, Siffert, Clark — **7**

8. **1970** Rindt, Ickx, Regazzoni, Brabham, Stewart, Rodriguez, Fittipaldi — **7**

9. **1974** Fittipaldi, Regazzoni, Scheckter, Lauda, Peterson, Reutemann, Hulme — **7**

10. **1976** Hunt, Lauda, Scheckter, Regazzoni, Andretti, Watson, Peterson — **7**

Three other years with seven race winners were 1979: Scheckter, G Villeneuve, Jones, Laffite, Regazzoni, Depailler, Jabouille; 1980: Jones, Piquet, Reutemann, Laffite, Pironi, Arnoux, Jabouille; 1981: Piquet, Reutemann, Jones, Laffite, Prost, Watson, G Villeneuve.

WINNERS FROM THE BACK OF THE GRID

When Kimi Räikkönen overtook Giancarlo Fisichella on the final lap of the 2005 Japanese Grand Prix, it seemed impossible that anyone could win after starting so far back on the grid (17th) – but they have. The chance of victory from outside the top ten starters is infinitesimal – it has only happened 18 times! Here, therefore, are the Top Ten who deserve a very special place in Grand Prix history, particularly John Watson who not only holds the record, but features twice in the top three! At Long Beach in March 1983, from a grid of 26 cars, John Watson started the race in 22nd spot – by modern standards, dead last! Just over 1 hour and 53 minutes of racing later, he took the chequered flag almost 30sec ahead of his McLaren teammate, Niki Lauda, who had started 23rd. During the race, the attrition rate had been high, but half of the large field recorded a finish and the McLarens were followed home by cars from the first and second rows of the grid. Winning from 22nd is truly exceptional – indeed, unique, as no driver before or since has won from outside the top 20 qualifiers.

1.	**JOHN WATSON** McLaren – 1983 Long Beach: was leading by lap 45 of 75	**22nd**
2.	**RUBENS BARRICHELLO** Ferrari – 2000 Hockenheim: Rubens' first win in a crazy race	**18th**
3.	**JOHN WATSON** McLaren – 1982 Detroit: Motown's first winner after a storming charge	**17th**
4.	**KIMI RÄIKKÖNEN** McLaren – 2005 Suzuka: Snatched the lead on final lap	**17th**
5.	**JACKIE STEWART** Tyrrell – 1973 Kyalami: Irresistibly took lead on lap 7 of 79	**16th**
6.	**MICHAEL SCHUMACHER** Benetton – 1995 Spa: Schumacher given suspended ban for blocking	**16th**
7.	**ALAN JONES** Shadow – 1977 Österreichring: Gave notice of his burgeoning talent	**14th**
8.	**JOHNNY HERBERT** Stewart – 1999 Nürburgring: Team Stewart's one and only victory	**14th**
9.	**BRUCE McLAREN** Cooper – 1960 Buenos Aires: Consistency won this race of attrition	**13th**
10.	**ALAIN PROST** Ferrari – 1990 Mexico: Prost at his stealthy best	**13th**

MOST GRAND SLAMS AND TRIPLE CROWNS

In sport, 'Grand Slam' normally conveys dominance. In Grand Prix it means a driver who takes pole position, leads every lap to win the race, and completes the rout by posting fastest lap. Expressed gastronomically, he devours the entire meal, leaving nothing on the table for his rivals but crumbs. In this age of pit-stop strategy and close competition between leading teams, the Grand Slam is comparatively rare, the last occasion being Fernando Alonso's 2005 French victory. Also Alain Prost, 'The Professor', notably during the turbo era, often engaged in racecraft which did not require him to win by front-running. So, for these reasons, this Top Ten lists Grand Slams together with Triple Crowns, the only distinction between the two being that for Triples, not every lap of the race was led. Numerically, Michael Schumacher heads the list, but the driver with the most dominant winning profile is Alberto Ascari. More than half his victories came this way, and most of those were Grand Slams. Jim Clark, the other Grand Slam aficionado, often drove away from the rest of the field as though in a different race. Between July 1962 and August 1965, he 'Grand Slammed' his opponents eight times within 31 races!

1. **MICHAEL SCHUMACHER**
24% of his 91 race victories were Slams or Crowns
22

2. **JIM CLARK**
44% of his 25 race victories were Slams or Crowns
11

3. **JUAN MANUEL FANGIO**
37% of his 24 race victories were Slams or Crowns
9

4. **ALAIN PROST**
16% of his 51 race victories were Slams or Crowns
8

5. **ALBERTO ASCARI**
54% of his 13 race victories were Slams or Crowns
7

6. **AYRTON SENNA**
17% of his 41 race victories were Slams or Crowns
7

7. **DAMON HILL**
27% of his 22 race victories were Slams or Crowns
6

8. **NIGEL MANSELL**
16% of his 31 race victories were Slams or Crowns
5

9. **MIKA HÄKKINEN**
25% of his 20 race victories were Slams or Crowns
5

10. **JACKIE STEWART**
15% of his 27 race victories were Slams or Crowns
4

Also with four Slams/Crowns were JACKY ICKX: 50% of 8 Race Victories, and FERNANDO ALONSO 21% of 19 Race Victories.

2.10

MOST VICTORIES IN A SEASON – DRIVERS

Expressed as a percentage, these are the ten drivers to have won the most races in a season, as usual excluding the Indianapolis 500-mile race. There was never a year when one driver won every championship race, although Alberto Ascari came mighty close in 1952, triumphing in all but one. Had he taken part in that opening round in Berne, it is more than likely he would have been victorious. In his absence, his Ferrari teammates lapped the rest of the field, scoring a resounding 1-2 finish. Ironically, he missed the Swiss GP because Enzo Ferrari wanted to take on the Americans, and entered Ascari for the Indy 500! It was an abortive attempt, Ascari's Ferrari 375 exiting early with mechanical ailments. Extreme single driver domination of 50% or more was a feature of the 1950s (see table), the trend undulating yet steadily declining over the sixties and seventies to reach a low point of just 12% by 1982. From there the trend gradually swung back, led by peaks in 1984 (44% Prost/McLaren) and 1988 (50% Senna/McLaren) and then on to Mansell and Williams in 1992. By the new millennium, Schumacher and Ferrari had reasserted 1950s-style single driver domination.

1. **ALBERTO ASCARI**
Ferrari – 1952: 6 victories from 7 championship rounds

86

2. **JUAN MANUEL FANGIO**
Maserati and Mercedes-Benz – 1954: 6 victories from 8 championship rounds

75

3. **MICHAEL SCHUMACHER**
Ferrari – 2004: 13 victories from 18 championship rounds

72

4. **JIM CLARK**
Lotus – 1963: 7 victories from 10 championship rounds

70

5. **JUAN MANUEL FANGIO**
Mercedes-Benz – 1955: 4 victories from 6 championship rounds

67

6. **MICHAEL SCHUMACHER**
Ferrari – 2002: 11 victories from 17 championship rounds

65

7. **ALBERTO ASCARI**
Ferrari – 1953: 5 victories from 8 championship rounds

63

8. **JIM CLARK**
Lotus – 1965: 6 victories from 10 championship rounds

60

9. **JUAN MANUEL FANGIO**
Maserati – 1957: 4 victories from 7 championship rounds

57

10. **NIGEL MANSELL**
Williams – 1992: 9 victories from 16 championship rounds

56

MOST VICTORIES IN A SEASON – TEAMS

Ferrari registers five times in this Top Ten of the most dominant teams in a season. Two are very recent, confirmation that the first five years of the new millennium evidenced the most sustained period of domination for car (Ferrari) and driver (Schumacher) in the history of the World Championship. In contrast, the two McLaren top ten entries were far more entertaining, each a hard fought championship between teammates. Unlike Ferrari's historical position, there are no team orders at McLaren. In 1984 Ron Dennis and designer John Barnard 'packaged' TAG, Lauda, Prost and Michelin to produce 12 victories. Four years later, Ron upped the ante to the astonishing level of 15 wins, including ten 1-2 finishes. Designer Gordon Murray, Honda, Senna, Prost and Goodyear were so very nearly victorious in all 16 rounds of the 1988 championship. Infamy haunts the race at Monza where leader Senna tripped over a slow Williams at the chicane just two laps from the chequered flag. It is said that Dennis experiences genuine pain when his team fails to win. What his emotions were that day in Italy is hard to imagine. He finds no deep satisfaction in merely winning – true fulfilment comes from supreme domination.

1. **ALFA ROMEO**
1950: Nino Farina 3 wins; Juan Manuel Fangio 3
100

2. **FERRARI**
1952: Alberto Ascari 6 wins; Piero Taruffi 1
100

3. **McLAREN**
1988: Ayrton Senna 8 wins; Alain Prost 7
94

4. **FERRARI**
1953: Alberto Ascari 5 wins; Mike Hawthorn 1; Nino Farina 1
88

5. **FERRARI**
2002: Michael Schumacher 11 wins; Rubens Barrichello 4
88

6. **MERCEDES-BENZ**
1955: Juan Manuel Fangio 4 wins; Stirling Moss 1
83

7. **FERRARI**
2004: Michael Schumacher 13 wins; Rubens Barrichello 2
83

8. **McLAREN**
1984: Alain Prost 7 wins; Niki Lauda 5
75

9. **WILLIAMS**
1996: Damon Hill 8 wins; Jacques Villeneuve 4
75

10. **FERRARI**
1956: Juan Manuel Fangio 3 wins; Peter Collins 2
71

MOST RACE VICTORIES AT MONACO

Nelson Piquet once described driving at Monaco as, 'Like riding a bike in your house.' The topography and narrowness of this iconic street circuit, surrounded by unforgiving barriers, brings out something utterly spell-binding in just a handful of drivers: they make their cars dance. With a Monaco master at the wheel, that mesmerising 'body language' of a car on a quick lap turns into a salsa of speed. Briefly down on its haunches, squirming under braking, then up on tip-toe to flick through a corner seeming to defy all rules of adhesion, the rear-end stepping out just a fraction to almost brush the barrier, skimming, wriggling, darting – all perfectly choreographed in a continuous blur of speed. Victory at Monaco is something special, and Ayrton Senna reigns supreme with more wins than any other. And to think that in 1988 he gifted one to Prost when he dropped it at Tabac with only 12 laps to go! That is just one of the myths and legends which is the magic of Monaco, which includes Graham Hill's extraordinary five wins record set in the sixties, and Moss vanquishing the three works Ferraris over 100 laps in 1961.

1.	**AYRTON SENNA** 1987, 1989, 1990, 1991, 1992 and 1993	6
2.	**GRAHAM HILL** 1963, 1964, 1965, 1968 and 1969	5
3.	**MICHAEL SCHUMACHER** 1994, 1995, 1997, 1999 and 2001	5
4.	**ALAIN PROST** 1984, 1985, 1986 and 1988	4
5.	**STIRLING MOSS** 1956, 1960 and 1961	3
6.	**JACKIE STEWART** 1966, 1971 and 1973	3
7.	**JUAN MANUEL FANGIO** 1950 and 1957	2
8.	**MAURICE TRINTIGNANT** 1955 and 1958	2
9.	**NIKI LAUDA** 1975 and 1976	2
10.	**JODY SCHECKTER** 1977 and 1979	2

Also with two Monaco victories were DAVID COULTHARD, 2000 & 2002 and FERNANDO ALONSO, 2006 & 2007.

MOST RACE VICTORIES AROUND THE NORDSCHLEIFE

In the annals of Grand Prix racing, the original Nürburgring, the Nordschleife, has legendary status. Many consider it to have been the ultimate test of a Grand Prix driver. An undulating road circuit, much of it tree-lined, with numerous blind brows and corners, finding any sort of driving rhythm was difficult, adding to the enormous powers of concentration required. Also playing on the mind was the simple fact that safety standards could not reach the accepted norm around its entire 14-mile length: seven Grand Prix drivers perished in their attempt to master the Nordschleife. Driving fast in this unique environment – fast enough to win and to beat others also seeking glory – required supreme confidence and enormous courage, especially in inclement weather, another frequent feature of the Eifel hills. It is little wonder that the term Ringmeister was coined to acknowledge the special status of those who had conquered the treacherous track and its cerebral devils. Only 15 drivers won the 22 World Championship races held on the Nordschleife. Five of them were very special, victorious more than once, but two of their number were unquestioned Grand Prix kings of the Nürburgring, Juan Manuel Fangio and John Young Stewart.

1.	**JUAN MANUEL FANGIO** 1954, 1956 and 1957	3
2.	**JACKIE STEWART** 1968, 1971 and 1973	3
3.	**ALBERTO ASCARI** 1951 and 1952	2
4.	**JOHN SURTEES** 1963 and 1964	2
5.	**JACKY ICKX** 1969 and 1972	2
6.	**NINO FARINA** 1953	1
7.	**TONY BROOKS** 1958	1
8.	**STIRLING MOSS** 1961	1
9.	**GRAHAM HILL** 1962	1
10.	**JIM CLARK** 1965	1

Also winners on the Nordschleife were 1966 JACK BRABHAM; 1967 DENNY HULME; 1974 CLAY REGAZZONI; 1975 CARLOS REUTEMANN; 1976 JAMES HUNT.

2.14

GREATEST WET-WEATHER VICTORIES

Imagine motorway driving in torrential rain. Standing water snatches at the steering wheel, which goes 'light' from aquaplaning, and traffic spray becomes impenetrable fog. Traditionally, Formula 1 races proceed in wet weather, albeit sometimes shortened, stopped/ restarted, or partially run under the safety car. Whichever, racing a Grand Prix car in the rain requires a mentality between heroism and recklessness, and to be ultimately victorious is an astonishing feat. But at the 14.1-mile Nordschleife, or the original 8.7-mile Spa-Francorchamps circuit, it is bravery itself, a quality given prominence in this Top Ten. Jackie Stewart's virtuoso performance at the 1968 German GP ranks above the rest. Due to accident injury, he drove with a wrist support for well over two hours, yet still won by more than four minutes. At the same race in 1962 Graham Hill raced for close-on three hours in streaming rain and under intense competitive pressure, the top three finishers separated by less than five seconds. The following year, but this time at Spa, Jim Clark's winning margin was rather more – close to five minutes, which demonstrated his superiority over 2½ hours of appalling race conditions.

1. **JACKIE STEWART**
Matra – 1968 Nürburgring: Victory by over 4 minutes
10

2. **STIRLING MOSS**
Lotus – 1961 Nürburgring: Conquered superior Ferraris
9

3. **JIM CLARK**
Lotus – 1963 Spa-Francorchamps: Victory by nearly 5 minutes
9

4. **ALBERTO ASCARI**
Ferrari – 1952 Spa-Francorchamps: Three hours of heavy rain at Spa!
8

5. **GRAHAM HILL**
BRM – 1962 Nürburgring: A streaming track and intense competition
8

6. **JEAN-PIERRE BELTOISE**
BRM – 1972 Monte Carlo: A virtuoso performance
7

7. **AYRTON SENNA**
Lotus – 1985 Estoril: His first victory was an astonishing display
7

8. **AYRTON SENNA**
McLaren – 1993 Donington: Was his opening lap the greatest ever driven?
6

9. **MICHAEL SCHUMACHER**
Ferrari – 1996 Catalunya: Made the rest look foolish
5

10. **LEWIS HAMILTON**
McLaren – 2008 Silverstone: Made the rest look foolish
5

3

ROOKIES AND JOURNEYMEN

The opening two chapters focussed chiefly on the glitz and glamour of F1 winners and champions. But what about the 500+ drivers who participated in the World Championship yet came away with little or no glory? Chapter 3 contrasts the two extremes in the lifecycle of the GP driver: the Rookie – arriving on the Grand Prix scene filled with youthful exuberance and promise – with that of the Journeyman – a competent, reliable but unexceptional performer, who had their chance but gained little genuine success, and have only memories to show for their efforts. Mediocrity may be too harsh a judgement to make of the Journeyman; you decide, but the juxtaposition with the Rookie is profound.

3.1

MOST STARTS DURING GP CAREER

During 2008, Rubens Barrichello was at the centre of some suitably directed fuss when he broke an F1 record which had stood for 15 years: the most GP starts by any driver. Ironically, Rubens' career began in the very same season that his predecessor, Ricardo Patrese retired. Remarkably, these two drivers cover a 30-year period, a time span which encompasses every other driver named in this list of GP career longevity. No one from the 1950s, 1960s or early 1970s makes this list (Graham Hill [1958-1975] being closest with 176 starts) because in those days drivers began their careers at a later age, far fewer races made up the World Championship series, and careers could frequently be abbreviated by death and injury, or retirement brought about by a desire for self-preservation. In today's comparatively safe racing environment, just as long as a driver can maintain motivation and continue delivering on the track – even when driving for a lesser team (Coulthard to Red Bull; Fisichella to Force India), it seems possible that a GP career these days could last fully 15 seasons. It seems unlikely that a further 15 years will pass before the record is wrested from Rubens.

1.	**RUBENS BARRICHELLO** 1993 to date: Jordan, Stewart, Ferrari, Honda	**264**
2.	**RICCARDO PATRESE** 1977-1993: Shadow, Arrows, Brabham, Alfa Romeo, Williams, Benetton	**256**
3.	**MICHAEL SCHUMACHER** 1991-2006: Jordan, Benetton, Ferrari	**249**
4.	**DAVID COULTHARD** 1994 to date: Williams, McLaren, Red Bull	**242**
5.	**GERHARD BERGER** 1984-1997: ATS, Arrows, Benetton, Ferrari, McLaren	**210**
6.	**ANDREA DE CESARIS** 1980-1994: Alfa Romeo, McLaren, Ligier, Minardi, Brabham, Rial, Dallara, Jordan, Tyrrell, Sauber	**208**
7.	**GIANCARLO FISICHELLA** 1996 to date: Minardi, Jordan, Benetton, Sauber, Renault, Force India	**208**
8.	**NELSON PIQUET** 1978-1991: Ensign, Brabham, Williams, Lotus, Benetton	**204**
9.	**JEAN ALESI** 1989-2001: Tyrrell, Ferrari, Benetton, Sauber, Prost, Jordan	**201**
10.	**ALAIN PROST** 1980-91 and 1993: McLaren, Renault, Ferrari, Williams	**199**

MICHELE ALBORETO also made 199 starts between 1981 & 1994 for Tyrrell, Ferrari, Larrousse, Arrows & Minardi.

MOST GP STARTS WITHOUT WINNING

The ten drivers listed on the preceding page all tasted success during their inordinately lengthy careers. They each won at least one Grand Prix – with the exception of just one, Andrea de Cesaris. His 200-plus races place the Roman sixth on the all-time starts ranking, more than enough to comfortably head this Top Ten and claim the unenviable title of the driver to have made the most GP starts without a win. Every young Rookie enters GP racing with a winning pedigree from karting and the lesser Formulae, and invariably upholds the belief that they can do the same in Formula 1. Most, if not all, on this list would have been considered likely winners at the start of their F1 journey, and of the current drivers Nick Heidfeld and Mark Webber can still expunge their names from this catalogue of frustration and disappointment. How can it be that Martin Brundle failed to win a Grand Prix, despite nearly – and perhaps that's the point – beating the great Ayrton Senna to the British Formula 3 title in 1983? But that is the fickle nature of F1, indeed of sport in general. Talent is not enough.

GP STARTS

1.	**ANDREA DE CESARIS** 1980-1994: Alfa Romeo, McLaren, Ligier, Minardi, Brabham, Rial, Dallara, Jordan, Tyrrell, Sauber	**208**
2.	**MARTIN BRUNDLE** 1984-1989 and 1991-1996: Tyrrell, Zakspeed, Williams, Brabham, Benetton, Ligier, McLaren, Jordan	**158**
3.	**DEREK WARWICK** 1981-1993: Toleman, Renault, Brabham, Arrows, Lotus, Footwork	**146**
4.	**NICK HEIDFELD** 2000 to date: Prost, Sauber, Jordan, Williams, BMW	**146**
5.	**JEAN-PIERRE JARIER** 1971 and 1973-1983: March, Shadow, Penske, Ligier, ATS, Lotus, Tyrrell, Osella	**134**
6.	**EDDIE CHEEVER** 1978 and 1980-1989: Theodore, Hesketh, Osella, Tyrrell, Ligier, Renault, Alfa Romeo, Lola, Arrows	**132**
7.	**PIERLUIGI MARTINI** 1984-85 and 1988-1995: Toleman, Minardi, Dallara	**118**
8.	**MARK WEBBER** 2002 to date: Minardi, Jaguar, Williams, Red Bull	**117**
9.	**MIKO SALO** 1994-200 and 2002: Lotus, Tyrrell, Arrows, BAR, Ferrari, Sauber, Toyota	**110**
10.	**PHILIPPE ALLIOT** 1984-1990 and 1993-94: RAM, Ligier, Lola, Larrousse, McLaren	**109**

MOST RACES LED WITHOUT WINNING

Heidfeld and Webber feature again in this Top Ten, both having come close to the possibility of victory by completing one of the essential prerequisites of winning – leading a race. In this era of pit-stop strategy, race leading has taken on a lesser importance, although that was not the case for all the drivers on this list. No artificiality about the races led by Jean Behra and Chris Amon who, on numerous occasions, led on merit. They each demonstrated their F1 race-winning ability in non-championship races, Amon twice, Behra no less than 12 times, but championship success eluded them. But they both came close. Behra led more than half of the 90 laps at the 1957 British GP until clutch trouble sidelined his 250F Maserati on lap 69. In 1967, Amon's Ferrari led every lap at St Jovite until transmission failure on lap 72 of 90. As others in this painful Top Ten could testify, such are the fortunes of GP racing. Frenchman 'Jumper' Jarier may only have led three times but, before car trouble intervened, two of these were from genuine race-winning positions. C'est la vie!

1. JEAN BEHRA
1952: Gordini 1; 1957: Maserati 3; 1958: BRM 1, Maserati 1; 1959: Ferrari 1

7

2. CHRIS AMON
1968: Ferrari 3; 1969: Ferrari 1; 1970: March 1; 1971: Matra 1; 1972: Matra 1

7

3. NICK HEIDFELD
2005: Williams 1; 2007: BMW 2; 2008: BMW 4

7

4. MARK WEBBER
2003: Jaguar 1; 2006: Williams 2; 2007: Red Bull 1

4

5. HARRY SCHELL
1954: Maserati 1; 1955: Maserati 1; 1956: Vanwall 1

3

6. EUGENIO CASTELLOTTI
1956: Ferrari 2; 1957: Ferrari 1

3

7. JACKIE OLIVER
1968: Lotus 1; 1970: BRM 1; 1973: Shadow 1

3

8. JEAN-PIERRE JARIER
1975: Shadow 2; 1978: Lotus 1

3

9. MASTEN GREGORY
1959: Cooper 2

2

10. ANDREA DE CESARIS
1982: Alfa Romeo 1; 1983: Alfa Romeo 1

2

Also leading two races but with no race wins were STEFAN JOHANSSON (1985 & 1986 Ferrari); DEREK WARWICK (1984 Renault & 1989 Arrows); IVAN CAPELLI (1988 March & 1990 Leyton House) and MIKA SALO (1999 Ferrari).

MOST RACES WITHOUT WINNING A POINT

Over the decades a category of driver has reached GP status less through talent than by wealth, their own or that of sponsors. Rather than any genuine expectation of glory, the motivation for these pay-drivers is the thrill and the privilege of participation at the highest level. Some in this Top Ten may therefore be totally philosophical about not even one championship point coming their way during their GP career. Luca Badoer, a driver with considerable ability, probably feels differently and maybe deserved better than to be heading up such a bleak Top Ten table. In the 1999 European GP, almost his final F1 start, Badoer's Minardi was holding fourth place when gearbox trouble intervened with just 13 laps to run. He was inconsolable, but maybe his salvation came from becoming the full-time test driver for Ferrari, a role he still holds today. No salvation for David Brabham, youngest of their illustrious father's three boys, and the only one to make a GP start. Or for Ricardo Rosset who claimed his 1999 Tyrrell was technically so inferior it had blighted his career. The team's response was to transpose the first and last letters of his surname when referring to him!

1.	**LUCA BADOER** 1993, 1995-96, and 1999: Lola, Minardi, Forti	**49**
2.	**BRETT LUNGER** 1975-1978: Hesketh, Surtees, March, McLaren, Ensign	**34**
3.	**TORA TAKAGI** 1998-99: Tyrrell, Arrows	**32**
4.	**MIKE BEUTTLER** 1971-1973: March	**28**
5.	**ENRIQUE BERNOLDI** 2001-02: Arrows	**28**
6.	**SCOTT SPEED** 2006-07: Toro Rosso	**28**
7.	**RICARDO ROSSET** 1996-1998: Arrows, Lola, Tyrrell	**27**
8.	**RUPERT KEEGAN** 1977-78, 1980, and 1982: Hesketh, Surtees, RAM, March	**25**
9.	**HUUB ROTHENGATTER** 1984-1986: Spirit, Osella, Zakspeed	**25**
10.	**DAVID BRABHAM** 1980 and 1994: Brabham, Simtek	**24**

TARSO MARQUES also made 24 'pointless' starts between 1996-97 & 2001 driving for Minardi.

LONGEST GAP BETWEEN RACE STARTS

A decade between GP starts is a surprising statistic, but diminutive Dutchman Jan Lammers accomplished it, competing in many forms of motor sport during the intervening years, including victory at Le Mans. American privateer Pete Lovely dipped a toe in the water in the early 1960s before a later more assiduous campaign when business interests allowed, by then well turned 40. Parallels may be drawn between the start/stop/start GP careers of Peter Revson, heir to the Revlon Cosmetics Empire, and Mike Hailwood, a World Champion motor cyclist. Teammates at Parnell Racing during their initial 1960s foray, they even shared the same flat. In the 1970s Hailwood returned in John Surtees' F1 team, while Revson joined McLaren via CanAm. Having gained a pair of victories, Revson left McLaren for Shadow for 1974, but was tragically killed in testing. Hailwood had taken over Revson's 1974 McLaren seat only to endure career-ending leg injuries – a road accident ending his life in 1981. In this unusual Top Ten, virtually every entry tells a tale, not forgetting Canadian Eppie Wietzes, who drove the first ever Safety Car. It was deployed at the 1973 Canadian GP – won by Pete Revson's McLaren.

1. JAN LAMMERS
Between 1982 French GP and 1992 Japanese GP
10:3

2. PETE LOVELY
Between 1960 US GP and 1969 Canadian GP
8:10

3. ANDRE PILETTE
Between 1956 French GP and 1964 Belgian GP
7:11

4. PETER REVSON
Between 1964 Italian GP and 1971 US GP
7:1

5. EPPIE WIETZES
Between 1967 Canadian GP and 1974 Canadian GP
7:1

6. MIKE HAILWOOD
Between 1965 Monaco GP and 1971 Italian GP
6:3

7. WOLFGANG SEIDEL
Between 1953 German GP and 1958 Belgian GP
4:9

8. ALEXANDER WURZ
Between 2000 Malaysian GP and 2005 San Marino GP
4:6

9. BRIAN HENTON
Between 1977 US West GP and 1981 Italian GP
4:5

10. ALEX ZANARDI
Between 1994 Australian GP and 1999 Australian GP
4:3

MOST FAILURES TO QUALIFY

Traditionally, Grand Prix qualifying exists not only to establish the formation of the starting grid. It also protects standards and ensures adequate safety levels by limiting the number of cars on track and the disparity in performance at each end of the grid. The popularity of Grand Prix in the 1980s meant that as many as 20 teams, twice that of today, turned up to race. This brought about pre-qualifying, a special one-hour session set aside at the unholy hour of 6.00am on the Friday morning. How demoralising for many teams and drivers to have to pack up and go home by 7.00am on the opening day of the race meeting! The Yamaha-powered West Zakspeed Racing team completed a full 16-race season of NPQs, but although the name of Zakspeed never graced a Grand Prix entry list again, the unfortunate driver with the blank starting record returned with a vengeance 17 years later. His name? Aguri Suzuki, founder of the late lamented Super Aguri Formula 1 team. Holding the DNQ (Did Not Qualify) record for the most failures is Italian Gabriele Tarquini. His 40 abortive attempts to qualify exceed by three the number of races he did start.

1. **GABRIELE TARQUINI**
1987-1995: 77 GPs entered with Osella, Coloni, AGS, Fondmetal, and Tyrrell
40

2. **BERTRAND GACHOT**
1989-1982 and 1994-95: 84 GPs entered with Onyx, Rial, Coloni, Jordan, Larrousse, and Pacific
37

3. **ROBERTO MORENO**
1982, 1987, 1989-1992 and 1995: 75 GPs entered with Lotus, AGS, Coloni, EuroBrun, Benetton, Andrea Moda, and Forti
32

4. **PIERCARLO GHINZANI**
1981, 1983-1989: 111 GPs entered with Osella, Toleman, Ligier, and Zakspeed
31

5. **ARTURO MERZARIO**
1972-1979: 84 GPs entered with Ferrari, Williams, Fittipaldi, March, Wolf, and Merzario
26

6. **BERND SCHNEIDER**
1988-1990: 34 GPs entered with Zakspeed and Arrows
25

7. **YANNICK DALMAS**
1987-1990 and 1994: 49 GPs entered with Larrousse Lola, AGS, and Larrousse
24

8. **STEFAN JOHANSSON**
1980 and 1983-1991: 103 GPs entered with Shadow, Spirit, Tyrrell, Toleman, Ferrari, McLaren, Ligier, Onyx, AGS, and Arrows
24

9. **ERIC VAN DE POELE**
1991-92: 29 GPs entered with Modena Lambo, Brabham, and Fondmetal
24

10. **NICOLA LARINI**
1987-92, 1994 and 1997: 49 GPs entered with Coloni, Osella, Ligier, Modena Lambo, Ferrari and Sauber
23

MOST RACE RETIREMENTS

Race retirements are broadly divided between those caused by car failure and those down to driver error. Even then, there are grey areas: did a car breakage result from driver mistreatment, or did mechanical failure cause the driver's accident? The third common reason is when a driver is inadvertently taken out by another's difficulties or miscalculation. Some hard-luck 'retirement' stories deserve their own special recognition. For example, the eight drivers whose World Championship careers lasted less than a single lap; Alex Soler-Roig, who holds the 'record' for the number of Grands Prix in which he took part – six – without ever finishing; Andrea de Cesaris, who retired from every single race in the 1987 season – 16; Rubens Barrichello of Brazil who joins Riccardo Patrese of Italy as holders of the 'record' for the number of retirements in their home Grand Prix – 10; and Barrichello again who, by virtue of his two dummy grid failures in 2002, joins de Cesaris and Jarno Trulli as the three drivers to have retired on more occasions than any other – 11 – before the completion of lap one.

And they say there is no such thing as luck!

1.	**ANDREA DE CESARIS** 1980-1994: 208 GP starts with Alfa Romeo, McLaren, Ligier, Minardi, Brabham, Rial, Dallara, Jordan, Tyrrell, and Sauber	**137**
2.	**RICCARDO PATRESE** 1977-1993: 256 GP starts with Shadow, Arrows, Brabham, Alfa Romeo, Williams, and Benetton	**130**
3.	**MICHELE ALBERTO** 1981-1994: 194 GP starts with Tyrrell, Ferrari, Larrousse, Arrows, and Minardi	**92**
4.	**NIGEL MANSELL** 1980-1992 and 1994-95: 187 GP starts with Lotus, Williams, Ferrari, and McLaren	**89**
5.	**RUBENS BARRICHELLO** 1993 to date: 264 GP starts with Jordan, Stewart, Ferrari, and Honda	**87**
6.	**GERHARD BERGER** 1984-1997: 210 GP starts with ATS, Arrows, Benetton, Ferrari, and McLaren	**86**
7.	**JACQUES LAFFITE** 1974-1986: 176 GP starts with Williams, and Ligier	**82**
8.	**JEAN ALESI** 1989-2001: 201 GP starts with Tyrrell, Ferrari, Benetton, Sauber, and Prost	**82**
9.	**NIKI LAUDA** 1971-1979 and 1982-1985: 171 GP starts with March, BRM, Ferrari, Brabham, and McLaren	**81**
10.	**NELSON PIQUET** 1978-1991: 204 GP starts with Ensign, McLaren (private), Brabham, Williams, Lotus, and Benetton	**80**

* Including DSQs and NCs.

3.8

MOST RACE VICTORIES IN FIRST SEASON

The media hype surrounding Lewis Hamilton in his Rookie season verged on hysteria. From seeing-off Massa at the very first corner in Australia, Hamilton's debut season was sensational: seven podiums on the trot; four race victories, the first only his sixth GP start; leading the championship battle for most of the season; beating his teammate, the reigning double World Champion, in the final points table, and ultimately to lose the championship by a single point – all the stuff to generate screaming tabloid headlines. Only Jacques Villeneuve has matched Lewis's triumphant Rookie year. Villeneuve possessed a sizeable reputation prior to his GP debut, being reigning US Indycar champion and Indy 500 winner. Once he got his hands on indubitably the best car in the 1996 field, the Williams-Renault FW15, great things were expected of the French-Canadian. But team-leader Damon Hill had other ideas, and saw-off Villeneuve's challenge. Even counting Farina and Fangio, already experienced GP pilots when the championship begin in 1950, Hamilton is only the ninth driver to win in his debut season.

1.	**JACQUES VILLENEUVE** 1996: European, British, Hungarian, and Portuguese GPs for Williams	**4**
2.	**LEWIS HAMILTON** 2007: Canadian, US, Hungarian, and Japanese GPs for McLaren	**4**
3.	**JUAN MANUEL FANGIO** 1950: Monaco, Belgian, and French GPs for Alfa Romeo	**3**
4.	**NINO FARINA** 1950: British, Swiss, and Italian GPs for Alfa Romeo	**3**
5.	**GIANCARLO BAGHETTI** 1961: French GP for Ferrari	**1**
6.	**JACKIE STEWART** 1965: Italian GP for BRM	**1**
7.	**CLAY REGAZZONI** 1970: Italian GP for Ferrari	**1**
8.	**EMERSON FITTIPALDI** 1970: US GP for Lotus	**1**
9.	**JUAN PABLO MONTOYA** 2001: Italian GP for Williams	**1**
10.		

YOUNGEST ROOKIE GP STARTER

Youth's relentless challenge of maturity creates a fascination with age in sport. The 'youngest ever' mantle is worn proudly by the latest bright young thing in most sporting arenas. As for driving talent, that natural and invisible ingredient which separates the great from the ordinary, these days it can burgeon at an indecently young age through that highly competitive sport of karting. Despite this, to find the youngest GP Rookie it is necessary to rewind almost 30 years. In 1980, Mike Thackwell blasted his Tyrrell from the Montreal grid where, at the very first corner, a clash with his teammate eliminated both on the spot. In 2007 a driver making a more auspicious debut also set an age-related record. Sebastian Vettel, substituting for Robert Kubica after his terrifying accident in Canada, brought his Sauber BMW home in eighth place. He was already only the sixth driver to make his GP debut under the age of 20, but by winning one championship point the young German also beat Jenson Button's equivalent benchmark from 2000. And the oldest GP driver? In 1955 Louis Chiron took the start aged almost 56 – little short of three times Thackwell's age on debut!

1.	**MIKE THACKWELL** Made debut at 1980 Canadian GP for Tyrrell	**19y** **5m 29d**
2.	**RICARDO RODRIGUEZ** Made debut at 1961 Italian GP for Ferrari	**19y** **6m 27d**
3.	**FERNANDO ALONSO** Made debut at 2001 Australian GP for Minardi	**19y** **7m 3d**
4.	**ESTEBAN TUERO** Made debut at 1998 Australian GP for Minardi	**19y** **10m 14d**
5.	**CHRIS AMON** Made debut at 1963 Belgian GP for Parnell Lola	**19y** **10m 20d**
6.	**SEBASTIAN VETTEL** Made debut at 2007 US GP for BMW	**19y** **11m 14d**
7.	**EDDIE CHEEVER** Made debut at 1978 South African GP for Hesketh	**20y** **1m 22d**
8.	**JENSON BUTTON** Made debut at 2000 Australian GP for Williams	**20y** **1m 22d**
9.	**TARSO MARQUES** Made debut at 1996 Brazilian GP for Minardi	**20y** **2m 12d**
10.	**PETER COLLINS** Made debut at 1952 Swiss GP for HWM	**20y** **6m 12d**

3.10

FEMALE FORMULA 1 DRIVERS

This is one of those rare Top Tens which cannot be fully populated. Just five women have entered the FIA Formula 1 World Championship, three of whom failed to qualify. Maria-Teresa de Filippis is rightly fêted as the first female driver in F1, but pride of place must go to her Italian compatriot Lella Lombardi, who achieved something many men have attempted yet failed. Lella won a (half) championship point in the foreshortened 1975 Spanish GP. Remember, in motor racing men and women normally compete directly and under exactly the same regulations. South African Desiré Wilson emulated Lombardi's feat by finishing sixth in her 1980 home GP, but this race became a casualty of the FISA/FOCA wars and was subsequently demoted from championship status. She does, however, own a place in the record books as the only female to actually win an F1 race, the Brands Hatch round of the 1980 Aurora F1 series. Will a female ever compete regularly for points, podiums or even wins in the macho world of Grand Prix? With talk of an F1 future following her first victory in the 2008 IRL series in the US, Danica Patrick might just be the one.

1. LELLA LOMBARDI
Between 1974 and 1976 entered 17 GPs making 12 starts; best result 6th

10

2. MARIA-TERESA DE FILIPPIS
In 1958-59 entered 5 GPs making 3 starts; best result 10th

7

3. DESIRÉ WILSON
In 1980 entered the British GP but failed to qualify

5

4. DIVINA GALICA
Between 1976 and 1978 entered 3 GPs but failed to qualify

2

5. GIOVANNA AMATI
In 1992 entered 3 GPs but failed to qualify

2

6.

7.

8.

9.

10.

DROVE MOST DIFFERENT MARQUES DURING CAREER

As with anything in life, chopping-and-changing is often a sign of frustration – surely the grass is greener? That certainly applies to some in this Top Ten, drivers harbouring deep self-belief, still searching for that elusive scenario which will bring long overdue success. At another level are those to whom team managers will turn should another stumble, able professionals like 'Supersub' Roberto Moreno, a safe pair of hands when a gap needed filling. Not to mention those so besotted with F1 that they will hang in there come what may, drive almost anything just to remain part of the F1 scene. Many of these multi-marque drivers are not GP winners, the notable exception being Moss. By the time Stirling eventually found his British winner in Vanwall, he had already driven six different marques, whereas Jacky Ickx, another winner, drove for a further four after his final Ferrari victory. But Chris Amon, if not a GP winner, is winner of this Top Ten by a street, having driven 13 different marques. This included his own Amon AF101-Cosworth which he qualified 24th but retired on lap 22 of 84 at the 1974 Spanish GP. Such tenacity to win is admirable and deserving of recognition.

1. **CHRIS AMON**
1963-1976: Lola, Lotus, Brabham, Cooper, Ferrari, March, Matra, Tecno, Tyrrell, Amon, BRM, Ensign, and Williams
13

2. **STIRLING MOSS**
1951-1961: HWM, ERA, Connaught, Cooper, Maserati, Mercedes-Benz, Vanwall, BRM, Lotus, and Ferguson
10

3. **MAURICE TRINTIGNANT**
1950-1964: Gordini, Ferrari, Vanwall, Bugatti, Cooper, Maserati, BRM, Aston Martin, Lotus, and Lola
10

4. **STEFAN JOHANSSON**
1980 and 1983-1991: Shadow, Spirit, Tyrrell, Toleman, Ferrari, McLaren, Ligier, Onyx, AGS, and Arrows
10

5. **ANDREA DE CESARIS**
1980-1994: Alfa Romeo, McLaren, Ligier, Minardi, Brabham, Rial, Dallara, Jordan, Tyrrell, and Sauber
10

6. **JACKY ICKX**
1966-1979: Matra, Cooper, Ferrari, Brabham, McLaren, Williams, Lotus, Ensign, and Ligier
9

7. **EDDIE CHEEVER**
1978 and 1980-1989: Theodore, Hesketh, Osella, Tyrrell, Ligier, Renault, Alfa Romeo, Lola, and Arrows
9

8. **ROBERTO MORENO**
1982, 1987, 1989-1992, and 1995: Lotus, AGS, Coloni, EuroBrun, Benetton, Jordan, Minardi, Andrea Moda, and Forti
9

9. **JO BONNIER**
1956-1971: Maserati, BRM, Porsche, Cooper, Brabham, McLaren, Honda, and Lotus
8

10. **JOHN SURTEES**
1960-1972: Lotus, Cooper, Lola, Ferrari, Honda, BRM, McLaren, and Surtees
8

Also driving for eight teams were JEAN-PIERRE JARIER between 1971 & 1973-1983 for March, Shadow, Penske, Ligier, ATS, Lotus, Tyrrell & Osella, and MARTIN BRUNDLE between 1984-1989 & 1991-1996 for Tyrrell, Zakspeed, Williams, Brabham, Benetton, Ligier, McLaren & Jordan.

MOST RACES WITH SAME TEAM

When Graham Hill sensationally departed BRM to rejoin Lotus for 1967, he was quoted as saying he was in danger of being 'painted over' if he remained any longer. Surely not the sentiment of Michael Schumacher – the longest-serving team driver ever – when he retired from Grand Prix racing after 72 wins from 162 GP starts with the Scuderia. In every long-term relationship there comes a time when one side or the other recognises it is over; time to move on. The difficulty arises when such realisation does not occur to both parties simultaneously! Not everyone in this Top Ten found better times after severing their long-term troth. Ayrton Senna, after six fruitful seasons with McLaren, switched to Williams in his search for probable success over likely failure. Tragically he was killed in only the third race for his new team. But his judgement had been sound, success for the Williams team continued whereas McLaren were not to win again for three years. He recognised the inherent danger in F1, openly admitting to a preference for death over debilitating injury. For one so pragmatic and success-driven, it is doubtful Senna would have had it any other way.

1. **MICHAEL SCHUMACHER**
Ferrari 1996-2006: 72 race victories, 5 drivers' and 6 constructors' championships
162

2. **DAVID COULTHARD**
McLaren 1996-2004: 12 race victories and 1 constructors' championship
150

3. **JACQUES LAFFITE**
Ligier 1976-1982 and 1985-86: 6 race victories
132

4. **MIKA HÄKKINEN**
McLaren 1993-2001: 20 race victories, 2 drivers' and 1 constructors' championship
131

5. **ALAIN PROST**
McLaren 1991 and 1984-1989: 30 race victories, 3 drivers' and 4 constructors' championships
107

6. **NELSON PIQUET**
Brabham 1978-1985: 13 race victories and 2 drivers' championships
106

7. **PIERLUIGI MARTINI**
Minardi 1985, 1988-1991, 1993-1995: No race victories; Best 4th
102

8. **RUBENS BARRICHELLO**
Ferrari 2000-2005: 9 race victories and 5 constructors' championships
102

9. **AYRTON SENNA**
McLaren 1988-1993: 35 race victories, 3 drivers' and 4 constructors' championships
96

10. **GERHARD BERGER**
Ferrari 1987-1989 and 1993-1995: 5 race victories
96

FASTEST AND FURTHEST

Speed, the very soul of Grand Prix racing. This chapter examines speed in F1, including the battle for pole position. Distance is another F1 fundamental, so Chapter 4 is not just about 'fastest', but also 'furthest'. Staying power has always been part of the Grand Prix game, indeed the original title given to World Championship-counting Grands Prix was 'Grand Epreuve', or 'great test'. In those early days the 'great test' was six or seven races lasting three hours or more. Today's TV-friendly version requires staying power of a different kind, shorter races but three times as many across the globe. Whichever era, winning championships demands massive reserves of physical and mental toughness.

MOST POLES DURING CAREER

The GP starting grid is formed by one of the great collective 'macho' events in the world of sport – F1 qualifying. It asks a fundamental question of its 20-plus participants: who can drive the fastest over a single flying lap? The balls-out unfettered shot at pole position – somewhat neutered these days by fuel strategy – is the opportunity for a driver, regardless of the outcome on race day, to demonstrate his superiority, his raw speed. In 2006, his final season, Michael Schumacher relieved Senna of his longstanding record for the number of pole positions. Senna had made this record his own in 1989, when he had first edged ahead of Jim Clark's 33, established way back in 1968. Senna had needed ten more race starts to reach Clark's record, but this was nothing compared with the additional 74 races required by Schumacher to match Senna's. So who is the king of qualifying when relating poles to starts? In the 'pole position' of pole positions sits Juan Manuel Fangio. Over his eight active seasons of racing, Fangio stuck it on pole better than once every second race, 57 per cent of the time.

1. **MICHAEL SCHUMACHER**
68 poles from 249 race starts, a 27% ratio
68

2. **AYRTON SENNA**
65 poles from 161 race starts, a 40% ratio
65

3. **JIM CLARK**
33 poles from 72 race starts, a 46% ratio
33

4. **ALAIN PROST**
33 poles from 199 race starts, a 17% ratio
33

5. **NIGEL MANSELL**
32 poles from 187 race starts, a 17% ratio
32

6. **JUAN MANUEL FANGIO**
29 poles from 51 race starts, a 57% ratio
29

7. **MIKA HÄKKINEN**
26 poles from 161 race starts, a 16% ratio
26

8. **NIKI LAUDA**
24 poles from 171 race starts, a 14% ratio
24

9. **NELSON PIQUET**
24 poles from 204 race starts, a 12% ratio
24

10. **DAMON HILL**
20 poles from 115 race starts, a 17% ratio
20

MOST POLES IN A SEASON

Little wonder Mansell mania swept Britain in 1992. The Isle-of-Man domiciled Brummie utterly dominated his championship season. He planted his Williams on pole in all but 2 of the 16 championship rounds, winning the first five races on the trot. Following two years at Ferrari, Mansell had returned to Williams with the promise of another genuine crack at that elusive title. Williams, now with Renault power, had designed and developed a car which took the application of electronic control mechanisms to new heights in the areas of suspension, gearbox, and traction. In 1992, the magnificent Patrick Head/Adrian Newey-designed Williams FW14B, which, relative to its opposition, many consider to be the most technologically sophisticated car of all time, combined reliability with dominant performance to realise Mansell's lifelong ambition. Many of Senna's great poles were recorded during the 1988-89 seasons when he was undoubtedly attempting to demoralise and humble Prost who was driving an identical McLaren. Prost (sort of) got his own back in 1993, taking over Mansell's seat in the astonishing Williams-Renault to equal Senna's 13 poles in a season.

1.	**NIGEL MANSELL** 1992: 14 poles from 16 race starts, an 88% ratio	**14**
2.	**AYRTON SENNA** 1988: 13 poles from 16 race starts, an 81% ratio	**13**
3.	**AYRTON SENNA** 1989: 13 poles from 16 race starts, an 81% ratio	**13**
4.	**ALAIN PROST** 1993: 13 poles from 16 race starts, an 81% ratio	**13**
5.	**MIKA HÄKKINEN** 1999: 11 poles from 16 race starts, a 69% ratio	**11**
6.	**MICHAEL SCHUMACHER** 2001: 11 poles from 16 race starts, a 69% ratio	**11**
7.	**AYRTON SENNA** 1990: 10 poles from 16 race starts, a 63% ratio	**10**
8.	**JACQUES VILLENEUVE** 1997: 10 poles from 17 race starts, a 59% ratio	**10**
9.	**RONNIE PETERSON** 1973: 9 poles from 15 race starts, a 60% ratio	**9**
10.	**NIKI LAUDA** 1974: 9 poles from 15 race starts, a 60% ratio	**9**

Also with nine poles were NIKI LAUDA in 1975 from 14 starts; NELSON PIQUET in 1984 from 16; DAMON HILL in 1996 from 16; MIKA HÄKKINEN in 1998 from 16, and MICHAEL SCHUMACHER in 2000 from 17.

MOST POLES AT HOME GRAND PRIX

Some say qualifying at your home Grand Prix is worth 0.2sec per lap, particularly for those in the hunt for pole position. No question, a home crowd is inspirational. The local boy on pole creates a fever-pitch atmosphere. In Brazil, where F1 passion generates its own fervour, Ayrton managed 6 poles from his 11 starts at Rio and Interlagos. With two each, Rubens and Felipe must be very proud to have carried his mantle this century. It also seems to bring something out in the British, with a country-leading 19 poles from 11 drivers, spearheaded by Clark's 5 from just 8 appearances. Strangely, Michael Schumacher never found the German GP an especially happy hunting ground, although he did claim three poles at the Nürburgring, close-by his place of birth, but winning or taking pole at the Luxemburg or European GP does not have nearly the same kudos. At another Mecca, Monza, just three Italians have seized pole, but the *Tifosi* are normally content just as long as it's a Ferrari. Of those 17 Ferrari poles, Ascari is the only Italian to oblige, but did so twice. But the French have the last laugh. Alain Prost holds the record for home wins – six!

1. AYRTON SENNA

Brazilian GP: 1986 Rio, Lotus; 1988 Rio, McLaren; 1989 Rio, McLaren; 1990 Interlagos, McLaren; 1991 Interlagos, McLaren; 1994 Interlagos, Williams

6

2. JIM CLARK

British GP: 1962 Aintree, Lotus; 1963 Silverstone, Lotus; 1964 Brands Hatch, Lotus; 1965 Silverstone, Lotus; 1967 Silverstone, Lotus

5

3. STIRLING MOSS

British GP: 1955 Aintree, Mercedes-Benz; 1956 Silverstone, Maserati; 1957 Aintree, Vanwall; 1958 Silverstone, Vanwall

4

4. NIKI LAUDA

Austrian GP: 1974 Österreichring, Ferrari; 1975 Österreichring, Ferrari; 1977 Österreichring, Ferrari

3

5. ALAIN PROST

French GP: 1983 Paul Ricard, Renault; 1988 Paul Ricard, McLaren; 1989 Paul Ricard, McLaren

3

6. NIGEL MANSELL

British GP: 1990 Silverstone, Ferrari; 1991 Silverstone, Williams; 1992 Silverstone, Williams

3

7. DAMON HILL

British GP: 1994 Silverstone, Williams; 1995 Silverstone, Williams; 1996 Silverstone, Williams

3

8. ALBERTO ASCARI

Italian GP: 1952 Monza, Ferrari; 1953 Monza, Ferrari

2

9. JUAN MANUEL FANGIO

Argentine GP: 1956 Buenos Aires, Ferrari; 1958 Buenos Aires, Maserati

2

10. MARIO ANDRETTI

US GP: 1968 Watkins Glen, Lotus; 1978 Watkins Glen, Lotus

2

Also with two home poles were RENE ARNOUX in 1981 at Dijon & 1982 at Paul Ricard with Renault, and with Ferrari, MICHAEL SCHUMACHER in 2002 & 2004 at Hockenheim and RUBENS BARRICHELLO in 2003 & 2004 and FELIPE MASSA in 2006 & 2007 both at Interlagos.

FEWEST RACES TO WIN FIRST POLE

Just imagine the outburst if, in 2007, Rookie Lewis Hamilton, qualifying for his very first GP, had stuck it on pole! It has happened, but only three times discounting Farina who was not a bona fide GP Rookie. Italian-born American Mario Andretti almost achieved the astonishing feat of pole in also his very last race 14 years later! On both occasions he was likely inspired by racing on home soil, but for his final pole – actually his penultimate race – the added incentive was driving for his beloved Ferrari. During his Italian childhood, his idol Alberto Ascari had been Ferrari-mounted. Argentinian Carlos Reutemann's debut pole also had fairy-tale qualities. He achieved it at the very first race of the season – at Buenos Aires. Like Andretti, French-Canadian Jacques Villeneuve came to Grand Prix following considerable open-wheel racing success Stateside, so a pole on debut was less of a shock than it might otherwise have proved. But it is still necessary to deliver, and Jacques did exactly that. Finally, imagine Valentino Rossi switching to F1 and taking pole on only his third appearance. That is exactly what that great world motor cycle champion John Surtees accomplished in 1960.

1. **NINO FARINA**
First pole at 1950 British GP, Silverstone driving an Alfa Romeo
1

2. **MARIO ANDRETTI**
First pole at 1968 US GP, Watkins Glen driving a Lotus
1

3. **CARLOS REUTEMANN**
First pole at 1972 Argentine GP, Buenos Aires driving a Brabham
1

4. **JACQUES VILLENEUVE**
First pole at 1996 Australian GP, Melbourne driving a Williams
1

5. **JUAN MANUEL FANGIO**
First pole at 1950 Monaco GP, Monte Carlo driving an Alfa Romeo
2

6. **EUGENIO CASTELLOTTI**
First pole at 1955 Belgian GP, Spa driving a Lancia
3

7. **JOHN SURTEES**
First pole at 1960 Portuguese GP, Oporto driving a Lotus
3

8. **MIKE PARKES**
First pole at 1966 Italian GP, Monza driving a Ferrari
4

9. **FROILAN GONZÁLEZ**
First pole at 1951 British GP, Silverstone driving a Ferrari
5

10. **STUART LEWIS-EVANS**
First pole at 1957 Italian GP, Monza driving a Vanwall
6

Fifty years after LEWIS-EVANS, LEWIS HAMILTON also took his first pole in his sixth race, the 2007 Canadian GP at Montréal, driving a McLaren.

MOST FASTEST LAPS DURING CAREER

Setting the fastest race-lap has always held a certain cachet in Grand Prix racing. In part this is because in the 1950s it gained an extra championship point, as it does in GP2 today. It's notable that Ayrton Senna does not appear in this Top Ten, whereas his nemesis Prost is at number two. This describes much about the differing winning strategies they each adopted. Strategy is also at the core of Michael Schumacher's massive total. With the aerodynamics of the contemporary Grand Prix car limiting on-track overtaking opportunities, pitstop strategy and related fuel and tyre tactics have become the primary route to victory. Schumacher and Ross Brawn's partnership at Ferrari made the Grand Prix race into a formulaic exercise. Brawn would call the strategy in the knowledge that, once given clean air, Schumacher could produce a succession of laps at qualifying pace. This would move him into a race-winning position by effectively overtaking the opposition during their pitstops. Jim Clark's record of quick race lappery was less through necessity. He was simply revelling in what he did best – driving a Formula 1 car exceedingly quickly with that silky deftness of a master at work.

ABOVE: *At number one for world title thrillers is 1976, a championship battle so compelling that it is often parodied as 'The greatest story ever told' (Top Ten 1.3). It was finally resolved between James Hunt and Niki Lauda by a single point (Top Ten 1.6), the pair shown on the podium at Jarama following the first victory of Hunt's ultimately successful campaign.*

BELOW: *Sir Stirling Moss enjoys special status as the most prolific Grand Prix winner never crowned World Champion (Top Ten 1.8). His first of sixteen victories was way back in 1955 at Aintree driving a Mercedes-Benz W196, famously beating Fangio by 0.2 seconds (Top Ten 6.2). Here the protagonists commence their race-long duel with Stirling on pole.*

ABOVE: *Lewis Hamilton hit the headlines in 2007 by winning his sixth ever Grand Prix. Amazingly that places him only tenth quickest for a maiden race victory (Top Ten 2.3). Ferrari driver Giancarlo Baghetti remains the only rookie ever to win on debut. At Reims in 1961 he saw off the works Porsches of Bonnier (10) and Gurney (12), winning by just 0.1 seconds (Top Ten 6.2).*

BELOW: *Victory at Monaco is something special, and Ayrton Senna reigns supreme. He heads that exceptional group of drivers who have triumphed more than once around the iconic Monte Carlo street circuit with its unforgiving barriers (Top Ten 2.12). For his fifth win in 1992, Senna (McLaren) had to work extremely hard to resist Mansell's hard charging Williams.*

ABOVE: *During 2008, Rubens Barrichello, already owner of one F1 record (Top Ten 2.4), exceeded the highest number of GP race starts, a milestone which had stood for fifteen years (Top Ten 3.1). Even after 250-plus races over sixteen Grand Prix seasons, and starting from sixteenth, Rubens was still good for a champagne-spraying podium at a wet Silverstone.*

BELOW: *Andrea de Cesaris tops more than one Top Ten, but for all the wrong reasons. He made more Grand Prix starts without winning than any other driver (Top Ten 3.2). He also retired from more races (Top Ten 3.7). But he had his moments. In 1983, his third full season, he took two second place finishes in his Alfa Romeo turbo (car 22), seen here at Kyalami.*

ABOVE: *In his 2007 debut season, Lewis Hamilton accepts the plaudits in Japan, flanked by Finns Räikkönen and Kovalainen. It was his fourth victory, equalling Jacques Villeneuve's rookie wins record (Top Ten 3.8). Although not destined to be the first ever rookie champion, few will forget Hamilton's sensational F1 entrance with seven straight podium finishes!*

BELOW: *Just five women have entered the FIA Formula 1 World Championship, three of whom did not qualify (Top Ten 3.10). Of the two who raced, Lella Lombardi achieved something many men have attempted yet failed, winning a (half) championship point in the foreshortened 1975 Spanish GP in her Lavazza March 751.*

ABOVE: *Little wonder Mansell Mania swept Britain in 1992, especially at Silverstone (pictured) where he won from his third successive home pole (Top Ten 4.3). Mansell utterly dominated his Championship season, planting his Williams on pole in all but two of the sixteen championship rounds (Top Ten 4.2) and winning the first five races on the trot (Top Ten 2.5).*

BELOW: *That most-raced of GP circuits, the Autodromo Nationale di Monza, features regularly in Formula 1 Top Tens (Top Ten 6.8). Fastest race (Top Ten 4.8); most race leaders (Top Ten 6.6); most lead changes (Top Ten 6.7)...on it goes. But the 1971 race, shown here, is the epitome, Peter Gethin's BRM recording the closest race finish ever (Top Ten 6.2).*

ABOVE: *Michael Schumacher's early domination of 21st century Formula 1 set numerous new records. Unsurprisingly he tops no less than twelve rankings, including the opening one (Top Ten 1.1). Another, however, reflects the negative aspect of this unparalleled career, Schumacher receiving the most race bans and disqualifications in F1 history (Top Ten 7.9).*

BELOW: *Poised, graceful, svelte, the Lotus 79, nicknamed Black Beauty, would look magnificent in any colour, but in JPS black and gold livery, it was definitely number one for stunning looks (Top Ten 5.11). Its 1978 on-track success also reaffirmed that well-known F1 maxim 'If it looks right, it is right'. Here the 79 is pictured winning on debut in Belgium in the hands of Mario Andretti.*

ABOVE: *The summit of F1 engine-power was reached between 1977-1988 through intensive development of turbo-charged engines (Top Ten 5.14). At least 1,000 bhp was available for races, and in qualifying trim, even 1,400 bhp was on tap, with spectacular results! Honda produced the most successful turbo, and here Mansell's Williams-Honda is pictured at Eau Rouge in 1986.*

BELOW: *From Hawthorn to Hamilton, Great Britain (or more accurately the UK) has been blessed with an abundance of Grand Prix winners and World Champions (Top Ten 6.3). Lewis is nineteenth in a list of World Championship Grand Prix winners which began fifty-five years ago with Mike Hawthorn's French Grand Prix Ferrari victory over Fangio's Maserati in 1953.*

ABOVE: *Despite outstanding work in safety, motor sport is dangerous. Once an F1 car loses control, the threat of death or serious injury can never be eliminated (Top Ten 7.11). The start, particularly the first corner, as depicted here at the 1989 French Grand Prix, remains the danger hot-spot (Top Ten 7.10). Remarkably in this case, all the drivers took the restart.*

BELOW: *The conclusion to this book courts controversy with the Top Ten all-time Formula 1 greats (Top Ten 7.12). Although, as with Senna, he was cut down at the height of his powers, that sublime Grand Prix driver Jimmy Clark takes top spot, pictured here at the 1967 US Grand Prix, first of the hat-trick of victories which closed his brilliant career in epitaphic style.*

1. **MICHAEL SCHUMACHER**
76 fastest laps from 249 race starts, a 31% ratio
76

2. **ALAIN PROST**
41 fastest laps from 199 race starts, a 21% ratio
41

3. **KIMI RÄIKKÖNEN**
34 fastest laps from 135 race starts, a 25% ratio
34

4. **NIGEL MANSELL**
30 fastest laps from 187 race starts, a 16% ratio
30

5. **JIM CLARK**
28 fastest laps from 72 race starts, a 39% ratio
28

6. **MIKA HÄKKINEN**
25 fastest laps from 161 race starts, a 16% ratio
25

7. **NIKI LAUDA**
24 fastest laps from 171 race starts, a 14% ratio
24

8. **JUAN MANUEL FANGIO**
23 fastest laps from 51 race starts, a 45% ratio
23

9. **NELSON PIQUET**
23 fastest laps from 204 race starts, an 11% ratio
23

10. **GERHARD BERGER**
21 fastest laps from 210 race starts, a 10% ratio
21

FURTHEST DISTANCE LED IN A SEASON

Two drivers command this table, each having led for over 2,000 miles during a season, the equivalent of ten Grand Prix distances! Nigel Mansell's one and only title in 1992 and Michael Schumacher's seventh and final championship 12 years later were, in absolute terms, the most dominant displays yet witnessed in World Championship history. Whilst Mansell is marginally behind on mileage, he is just ahead for the record number of laps led in a season, 693. But neither are as proportionately dominant as Jim Clark in 1963 or Alberto Ascari in 1952, both of whom led for more than 70 per cent of the race distances over those seasons, albeit when far fewer championship races were staged compared with today. The other major difference was that Ascari's Ferrari 500 and Clark's Lotus 25 were designed to last a full race distance without the need to pit for fuel or tyres. Once they were ahead they stayed there, the Italian leading start-to-finish four times from his six victories in 1952 and Clark six from seven in 1963. But ultimately, seven-times World Champion Michael Schumacher stamps his authority on this Top Ten, making five separate entries, including top spot.

1.	**MICHAEL SCHUMACHER** 2004: Led 16 of the 18 rounds for 683 laps, being 61% of the season's race distance	**2,085**
2.	**NIGEL MANSELL** 1992: Led 14 of the 16 rounds for 693 laps, being 68% of the season's race distance	**2,043**
3.	**MICHAEL SCHUMACHER** 2002: Led 13 of the 17 rounds for 558 laps, being 53% of the season's race distance	**1,718**
4.	**JIM CLARK** 1963: Led 9 of the 10 rounds for 506 laps, being 72% of the season's race distance	**1,714**
5.	**MICHAEL SCHUMACHER** 1994: Led 13 of the 16 rounds for 629 laps, being 57% of the season's race distance	**1,703**
6.	**MIKA HÄKKINEN** 1998: Led 12 of the 16 rounds for 576 laps, being 56% of the season's race distance	**1,683**
7.	**AYRTON SENNA** 1988: Led 12 of the 16 rounds for 553 laps, being 56% of the season's race distance	**1,652**
8.	**MICHAEL SCHUMACHER** 2000: Led 14 of the 17 rounds for 548 laps, being 50% of the season's race distance	**1,609**
9.	**MICHAEL SCHUMACHER** 2001: Led 13 of the 17 rounds for 533 laps, being 49% of the season's race distance	**1,562**
10.	**ALBERTO ASCARI** 1952: Led 6 of the 7 rounds for 348 laps, being 77% of the season's race distance	**1,458**

FURTHEST DISTANCE RACED FOR THE CHAMPIONSHIP

Formula 1 has become a TV sport attracting millions as the story of the World Championship unfolds year-by-year. It is through television that each Grand Prix promotes its host countries or city to the global tourist marketplace. With a waiting list of countries eager to join Bernie's F1 circus, little wonder there is pressure for a 20-race calendar. In the 1960s, ten World Championship races each year became the norm, compared with just six when the championship began in 1950 (excluding the Indy 500). But, as the number of races increased, their duration reduced from a minimum of 500km (310 miles) or three hours in the 1950s, to today's maximum of 305km (189.52 miles) or two hours, whichever shorter. By the close of the 1970s the number of races had risen to around 16, where it settled until more recently. As the table shows, the season to first reach 17 races was 1977, the year following 'The greatest story ever told'. The titanic struggle for the 1976 championship was the catalyst that turned an extravagant minority sport into a global TV extravaganza.

1.	**2005** 19 championship rounds across Europe (11), the Americas (3), rest of the world (5)	**3,592**
2.	**2006** 18 championship rounds across Europe (10), the Americas (3), rest of the world (5)	**3,405**
3.	**2004** 18 championship rounds across Europe (10), the Americas (3), rest of the world (5)	**3,401**
4.	**2002** 17 championship rounds across Europe (11), the Americas (3), rest of the world (3)	**3,216**
5.	**2000** 17 championship rounds across Europe (11), the Americas (3), rest of the world (3)	**3,216**
6.	**1995** 17 championship rounds across Europe (11), the Americas (3), rest of the world (3)	**3,212**
7.	**2007** 17 championship rounds across Europe (9), the Americas (3), rest of the world (5)	**3,212**
8.	**1977** 17 championship rounds across Europe (10), the Americas (5), rest of the world (2)	**3,199**
9.	**2001** 17 championship rounds across Europe (11), the Americas (3), rest of the world (3)	**3,178**
10.	**1997** 17 championship rounds across Europe (12), the Americas (3), rest of the world (2)	**3,133**

FASTEST RACE-WINNING SPEEDS

The average speed around all 19 circuits used during the 2005 championship – the final year of unrestricted V10 engines – was almost 126mph! That is 40 per cent higher than the slowest equivalent statistic, the 90mph average of half-a-century earlier (1957). Although an imperfect comparison, it is indicative of relative performance levels. The maximum velocity of a 1950s F1 car was not so very different from today, but with superior acceleration resulting from more traction with less drag, coupled with phenomenal braking, the straight-line performance of the contemporary F1 car is truly spectacular. But even that pales against the cornering powers available today through aero downforce. Take the high-speed Monza circuit. The 1971 race, the first won at an average speed exceeding 150mph, still ranks as the fifth fastest Grand Prix of all time. Chicanes and other measures meant that 32 years passed before the Monza victor came home at a faster race average. It is important to appreciate that, to achieve this, 2003-winner Michael Schumacher negotiated the Lesmo and Parabolica corners at speeds totally unimaginable to the 1971 winner, Peter Gethin.

SPEED MPH

1.	**2003 ITALIAN GP** Monza: winner Michael Schumacher, Ferrari	**153.843**
2.	**2005 ITALIAN GP** Monza: winner Juan Pablo Montoya, McLaren	**153.539**
3.	**2006 ITALIAN GP** Monza: winner Michael Schumacher, Ferrari	**152.742**
4.	**2004 ITALIAN GP** Monza: winner Rubens Barrichello, Ferrari	**151.847**
5.	**1971 ITALIAN GP** Monza: winner Peter Gethin, BRM	**150.755**
6.	**1970 BELGIAN GP** Spa-Francorchamps: winner Ricardo Rodriguez, BRM	**149.942**
7.	**2002 ITALIAN GP** Monza: winner Rubens Barrichello, Ferrari	**149.806**
8.	**1993 ITALIAN GP** Monza: winner Damon Hill, Williams	**148.597**
9.	**2001 ITALIAN GP** Monza: winner Juan Pablo Montoya, Williams	**148.572**
10.	**1997 ITALIAN GP** Monza: winner David Coulthard, McLaren	**147.909**

4.9

FURTHEST WINNING MARGINS

In 1979 Niki Lauda quit GP racing to set up LaudaAir. The great Austrian walked out during practice for the Canadian GP uttering, 'I am tired of driving round and round in circles!' Later he retracted his slur on F1 in the best possible way by returning to win a third world crown. His parting words alluded to the unavoidable fact that Grand Prix is raced over so-many laps of a given circuit. Inevitably, the leader begins to encounter 'traffic', and by passing these slower cars 'laps' them. On 22 occasions, the winning driver has 'lapped' the entire field, but only two drivers have ever lapped the field twice, Damon Hill the most recent. Besides these two mighty achievements by Jackie and Damon, time must be used to separate the remainder of this Top Ten. The longest same lap winning margins relate to the extreme lap distances for the original Nürburgring and Spa circuits, along with Pescara. Apart, that is, from the bizarre happenings at the 1958 Portuguese Grand Prix when Mike Hawthorn, almost a lap behind Stirling Moss but immediately ahead on the road, spun his Ferrari while completing his final lap, taking many minutes to regain the track.

1.	**JACKIE STEWART** 1969 Spanish GP, Montjuïc	**2 laps**
2.	**DAMON HILL** 1995 Australian GP, Adelaide	**2 laps**
3.	**STIRLING MOSS** 1958 Portuguese GP, Oporto	**5min 12.75sec**
4.	**JIM CLARK** 1963 Belgian GP, Spa-Francorchamps	**4min 54sec**
5.	**JACKIE STEWART** 1968 German GP, Nürburgring	**4min 3.2sec**
6.	**TONY BROOKS** 1958 German GP, Nürburgring	**3min 29.7sec**
7.	**STIRLING MOSS** 1957 Pescara GP, Pescara, Italy	**3min 13.9sec**
8.	**NINO FARINA** 1951 Belgian GP, Spa-Francorchamps	**2min 51sec**
9.	**ALBERTO ASCARI** 1953 Belgian GP, Spa-Francorchamps	**2min 48.2sec**
10.	**PIERO TARUFFI** 1952 Swiss GP, Berne	**2min 37.2sec**

THE TOP TEN FASTEST RACE TRACKS

These are the Top Ten fastest motor racing circuits from the 63 tracks to have staged a GP race. As many have been radically altered over time, this table portrays the fastest officially-recorded qualifying or race lap at that specific venue. With speed the soul of GP racing, it is appropriate that topping the table is that cathedral to speed, *Autodromo Nationale di Monza*. Its reputation as a high-speed circuit was further enhanced by the use of banking in the 1950s and 1960s, but it was in 2002 that Monza became one of just two tracks where lap speed exceeded 160mph. Prior to that, Silverstone alone held the 'fastest circuit' record. In 1985, Keke Rosberg manhandled his spitting and snarling Williams FW10 Honda round Silverstone in just 65 seconds to take pole at an average speed of 160.925mph! It was a shocking moment when rulemakers realised that turbocharged cars demanded significant speed-restricting track alterations. And if that image doesn't raise goosebumps, just imagine Chris Amon lapping the long Spa circuit in a 1970s March at 152.077mph, or Tony Brooks' Ferrari averaging 149.129mph at the AVUS in 1959. Just suppose a tyre had delaminated or the suspension had let go!

1.	**MONZA** 2004 Italian GP: pole Rubens Barrichello, Ferrari	**161.802**
2.	**SILVERSTONE** 1985 British GP: pole Keke Rosberg, Williams	**160.925**
3.	**ÖSTERREICHRING** 1987 Austrian GP: pole Nelson Piquet, Williams	**159.457**
4.	**HOCKENHEIM** 1991 German GP: pole Nigel Mansell, Williams	**156.722**
5.	**SPA-FRANCORCHAMPS** 1970 Belgian GP: fastest lap Chris Amon, March	**152.077**
6.	**AVUS** 1959 German GP: fastest lap Tony Brooks, Ferrari	**149.129**
7.	**KYALAMI** 1985 South African GP: pole Nigel Mansell, Williams	**147.202**
8.	**REIMS** 1966 French GP: pole Lorenzo Bandini, Ferrari	**145.313**
9.	**SUZUKA** 2002 Japanese GP: pole Michael Schumacher, Ferrari	**142.593**
10.	**MELBOURNE** 2004 Australian GP: fastest lap Michael Schumacher, Ferrari	**141.010**

Chapter

5

CARS AND TEAMS

'The fusion of human skill with technological excellence.' This is the elemental mix of Grand Prix racing. While the drivers take the glory, the team-owners wield the power and, as with the great football teams, Grand Prix cars and teams attract their own special following. In recognition of these two fundamentals within Grand Prix racing – driver and car; human and technical – parallel championships operate in Formula 1: the Drivers' World Championship and the World Championship for Constructors. Chapter 5 is a tribute to the latter, to the blood sweat and tears and technological excellence which got their man first to the chequered flag, or simply got him to the start line!

MOST GP PARTICIPATIONS BY TEAM

At first glance, only three currently-active GP teams feature in this Top Ten, until it is remembered that Tyrrell begat BAR, which spawned Honda; Toro Rosso is effectively Minardi by another name; and Benetton morphed into Renault. So the continued existence of the top three teams – 'the Big 3' – is a tribute to Enzo Ferrari, Ron Dennis, and Sir Frank Williams. Of course, Enzo Ferrari is long gone (1900-1983) and Ron Dennis did not found his team (Bruce McLaren 1935-1970), but as many great names have come and gone – Alfa Romeo, Maserati, Cooper, BRM, Vanwall – 'the Big 3' have maintained an important continuity for the success and growth of GP racing. They are also responsible for some of the most fabled inter-team rivalries on the circuits of the world. One other Grand Prix stalwart on this list, sadly moribund, also deserves special mention: Team Lotus. Founded by the late, great Colin Chapman (1928-1982), Lotus was the team to beat in the 1960s and 1970s, with a succession of formidable drivers attracted by race-winning technical innovations from the fertile mind of the marque's inspirational leader. Jim Clark, Graham Hill, Jochen Rindt, and Mario Andretti all won titles with Chapman's team.

1.	**FERRARI** First race: 1950 Monaco GP; Last race: Active team	**771**
2.	**McLAREN** First race: 1966 Monaco GP; Last race: Active team	**644**
3.	**WILLIAMS** First race: 1972 British GP; Last race: Active team	**556**
4.	**LOTUS** First race: 1958 Monaco GP; Last race: 1994 Australian GP	**491**
5.	**TYRRELL** First race: 1970 Canadian GP; Last race: 1998 Japanese GP	**430**
6.	**BRABHAM** First race: 1962 German GP; Last race: 1992 Hungarian GP	**394**
7.	**ARROWS** First race: 1978 Brazilian GP; Last race: 2002 German GP	**382**
8.	**MINARDI** First race: 1985 Brazilian GP; Last race: 2005 Chinese GP	**340**
9.	**LIGIER** First race: 1976 Brazilian GP; Last race: 1996 Japanese GP	**279**
10.	**BENETTON** First race: 1986 Brazilian GP; Last race: 2001 Japanese GP	**260**

MOST CONSTRUCTORS' CHAMPIONSHIPS

'The Big 3' again dominate this Top Ten. The Constructors' Championship began in 1958 eight years after the drivers' contest. Over the following 50 years, these three teams have taken almost two-thirds of the constructor's titles. Since McLaren's first title in 1974 (pre-Ron Dennis), 'the Big 3' have only failed to scoop honours on four occasions (1978 Lotus; 1995 Benetton; 2005 and 2006 Renault). From 1984 to 1999 – with Ferrari barely featuring at times – McLaren and Williams redefined the dynamics of winning in Grands Prix, each taking seven championship titles. The supremacy of the two British teams caused Gianni Agnelli, head of Ferrari's owners FIAT, to charge Luca di Montezemolo with the task of returning Ferrari to championship-winning form, thus the formation of the Ferrari super-team under Jean Todt. With Ross Brawn, Rory Byrne, Michael Schumacher, and many others, this group eventually found the key to sustained success, taking six constructor's titles in a row from 1999. With the failure of their relationship with BMW, the great days for Williams may now be gone. So far this century, Williams have not won a championship, but, for that matter, neither have McLaren!

		CHAMPIONSHIPS
1.	**FERRARI** 1961, 1964, 1975-1977, 1979, 1982-83, 1999-2004, 2007	15
2.	**WILLIAMS** 1980-81, 1986-87, 1992-1994, 1996-97	9
3.	**McLAREN** 1974, 1984-85, 1988-1991, 1998	8
4.	**LOTUS** 1963, 1965, 1968, 1970, 1972-73, 1978	7
5.	**COOPER** 1959-60	2
6.	**BRABHAM** 1966-67	2
7.	**RENAULT** 2005-06	2
8.	**VANWALL** 1958	1
9.	**BRM** 1962	1
10.	**MATRA** 1969	1

The only other Constructors' Champions were TYRRELL in 1971 and BENETTON in 1995.

MOST SUCCESSFUL WINNING TEAMS

The 2007 season saw Ferrari become the first constructor to win 200 races. A terrific achievement, yes, but the Scuderia does enjoy an advantage. It is the only team to have participated in every one of the 59 championship seasons; a proud claim indeed. McLaren entered 16 years after Ferrari, Bruce himself taking their inaugural victory in 1968. By then, Ferrari had notched up 41. Even so, McLaren's success was immense, especially from 1981 under the stewardship of Ron Dennis. By 1993 their wins count exceeded Ferrari's – by one (104 v. 103). Frank Williams first became a constructor in 1972, eventually breaking into the winner's circle in 1979. His battle for supremacy with Ron Dennis is legendary; the poaching – er, exchanging – of engine deals, sponsors, and even drivers from one another just part of the story. Head-to-head as team principals between 1981 and 1999 – before the Ferrari/Schumacher steamroller usurped both British teams – Sir Frank posted 92 victories to Ron's 99, each figure a massive tribute to a pair of young penniless Brits who forever will stand as the greatest team entrepreneurs the ruthless world of F1 has seen – and both inveterate racers to boot!

1.	**FERRARI** 1950s 29; 1960s 13; 1970s 37; 1980s 18; 1990s 28; 2000s 83	**208**
2.	**McLAREN** 1950s NA; 1960s 4; 1970s 20; 1980s 56; 1990s 43; 2000s 38	**161**
3.	**WILLIAMS** 1950s NA; 1960s NA; 1970s 5; 1980s 37; 1990s 61; 2000s 10	**113**
4.	**LOTUS** 1950s 0; 1960s 26; 1970s 25; 1980s 8; 1990s 0	**79**
5.	**BRABHAM** 1950s NA; 1960s 12; 1970s 8; 1980s 15; 1990s 0	**35**
6.	**RENAULT** 1950s NA; 1960s NA; 1970s 1; 1980s 14; 1990s NA, 2000s 10	**33**
7.	**BENETTON** 1950s NA; 1960s NA; 1970s NA; 1980s 2; 1990s 25; 2000s 0	**27**
8.	**TYRRELL** 1950s NA; 1960s NA; 1970s 21; 1980s 2; 1990s 0	**23**
9.	**BRM** 1950s 1; 1960s 12; 1970s 4	**17**
10.	**COOPER** 1950s 7; 1960s 9	**16**

MARQUES WHICH NEVER WON A RACE

If there is a Top Ten table which illustrates the challenge of winning in F1, this is it. Arrows entered GP racing in 1978 with much promise, and raced over 25 seasons before the team was wound up in 2002. And how closely they brushed with success – Ricardo Patrese leading their third-ever race at Kyalami with just 15 laps remaining, whereas Damon Hill had begun the final lap in the lead at the Hungaroring in 1997 – mechanical ailments responsible for both near misses. But it's not just the independent F1 teams which have tried and failed. The appearance of the world's largest car manufacturer, Toyota, demonstrates that even unlimited financial and technological resources guarantee nothing in F1. Now in their seventh season, Toyota may have taken the more challenging organic route, whereas other manufacturers have entered via acquisition of an established team. Yet they too have found F1 a hard nut to crack. Honda's singleton victory is scant reward since taking total ownership of BAR at the end of 2005, and BMW have only just met success in their third year with Sauber. Remember, Ford withdrew their Jaguar F1 team after just five years (85 Grands Prix) of fruitless effort.

1. **ARROWS**
First race: 1978 Brazilian GP; Last race: 2002 German GP

382

2. **MINARDI**
First race: 1985 Brazilian GP; Last race: 2005 Chinese GP

340

3. **SAUBER**
First race: 1993 South African GP; Last race: 2005 Chinese GP

215

4. **OSELLA**
First race: 1980 Brazilian GP; Last race: 1990 Australian GP

151

5. **LOLA**
First race: 1962 Dutch GP; Last race: 1993 Portuguese GP

149

6. **SURTEES**
First race: 1970 British GP; Last race: 1978 Canadian GP

118

7. **TOYOTA**
First race: 2002 Australian GP; Last race: Active team

118

8. **BAR**
First race: 1999 Australian GP; Last race: 2005 Japanese GP

117

9. **FITTIPALDI**
First race: 1975 Argentine GP; Last race: 1982 Italian GP

104

10. **ENSIGN**
First race: 1973 French GP; Last race: 1982 Italian GP

99

5.5

CONSTRUCTORS WHO RACED THEIR OWN CAR

The 1960/70s were the heyday for the driver/constructor, a F1 phenomenon inspired by the ubiquitous Ford Cosworth DFV V8. Brabham, McLaren, and Gurney did not initially use the DFV route, yet are the only three of the genre to taste victory at the wheel of their own car. Fascinatingly, the GP careers of these three very special F1 people are entwined. Antipodeans Jack Brabham and Bruce McLaren were teammates at Cooper between 1959 and 1961, following which Jack departed to set up his own racing team, Bruce emulating him four years later. Brabham's lead driver was American Dan Gurney, their three-season partnership bringing only modest success. But in 1966 Brabham led his team to back-to-back titles, ironically after the loyal Gurney had departed – to set up his own racing team! And only 20 World Championship races later, at Spa-Francorchamps in 1968, Bruce McLaren became the second winner in a car bearing his own name – although he was not the second driver to win in his own car. That feat was claimed by Dan Gurney, whose beautiful Eagle-Weslake also triumphed at Spa, one year before McLaren's victory.

1.	**FITTIPALDI** 1975-1980, brother Wilson made 10 starts and Emerson 74, best race finish 2nd	**84**
2.	**BRABHAM** 1962-1970, Jack won 7 GPs taking the drivers' championship in 1966 and constructors' titles in 1966-67	**80**
3.	**McLAREN** 1966-1970, Bruce was victorious in 1968	**33**
4.	**EAGLE (GURNEY)** 1966-1968, Dan also won just the once, in 1967	**24**
5.	**SURTEES** 1970-1972, Big John's best finish was 5th	**19**
6.	**MERZARIO** 1978-1979, but Arturo never made the finishing line	**10**
7.	**GORDINI** 1951 French GP, Amédée qualified his Simca Gordini but retired	**1**
8.	**ASTON** 1952 German GP, Bill qualified his Aston-Butterworth but retired	**1**
9.	**AMON** 1974 Spanish GP, Chris qualified but retired	**1**
10.	**REBAQUE** 1979 Canadian GP, Hector qualified but retired	**1**

Failure to qualify his own car at his favoured circuit, Monaco, in 1975 led to Graham Hill's decision to retire from F1.

DRIVERS WHO WON FOR FERRARI

The top three fittingly represent the most successful periods for The Prancing Horse in the early 1950s, the mid-1970s, and the recent domination which opened the 21st century. Dwarfing the tally for all other drivers is Schumacher's extraordinary 72 victories realised over his 11 seasons at the Scuderia. During that time his three teammates – Eddie Irvine, Rubens Barrichello and Felipe Massa – accumulated just 14 wins between them! Schumacher is responsible for more than one-in-three of the 206 Ferrari Grand Prix victories accrued since 1951, and which were accounted for by 36 drivers from 13 nationalities. British and French drivers are very much to the fore, together with – Italians. Including Luigi Musso's shared victory with Fangio, eight Italians have enjoyed that very special moment of winning a Grand Prix in their beloved Ferrari, with three of their number – Farina, Ascari, and Scarfiotti – doing so at Monza! And lest we forget, Italian-born American Mario Andretti won on his Ferrari debut! The hall of fame for British Ferrari winners is John Surtees and Eddie Irvine (4), Mike Hawthorn, Peter Collins, and Nigel Mansell (3), plus Tony Brooks (2).

1. **MICHAEL SCHUMACHER**
1996: 3; 1997: 5; 1998: 6; 1999: 2; 2000: 9 (World Champion);
2001: 9 (World Champion); 2002: 11 (World Champion); 2003: 6 (World Champion); 2004: 13 (World Champion); 2005: 1, 2006: 7

72

2. **NIKI LAUDA**
1974: 2; 1975: 5 (World Champion); 1976: 5; 1977: 3 (World Champion)

15

3. **ALBERTO ASCARI**
1951: 2; 1952: 6 (World Champion); 1953: 5 (World Champion)

13

4. **FELIPE MASSA**
2006: 2, 2007: 3, 2008 5 to date

10

5. **RUBENS BARRICHELLO**
2000: 1; 2002: 4; 2003: 2; 2004: 2

9

6. **KIMI RÄIKKÖNEN**
2007: 6 (World Champion); 2008: 2 to date

8

7. **JACKY ICKX**
1968: 1; 1970: 3; 1971: 1; 1972: 1

6

8. **GILLES VILLENEUVE**
1978: 1; 1979: 3; 1981: 2

6

9. **CARLOS REUTEMANN**
1977: 1; 1978: 4

5

10. **ALAIN PROST**
1990: 5

5

GERHARD BERGER also won five times for Ferrari, twice in 1987 and also 1988, 1989 & 1994.

DRIVERS WHO WON FOR McLAREN

The two drivers heading this Top Ten underwrote a decade of McLaren dominance. Both spent six-year stints with the team, two as teammates. Prost became the driving force from 1984, bringing a hat-trick of championships, one nabbed by teammate Lauda. After Prost's departure, Senna claimed two more, and neatly, in their spell together, shared championship honours one apiece. That was the only sharing in what became the most fêted intra-team rivalry ever known. Together they made 32 starts, Senna shading Prost 14 wins to 11. More telling was that in the 20 races in which they both finished, it was 14 to 6. The next two, Häkkinen and Coulthard, were teammates of a different breed who prospered with the Mercedes-Benz association which began in 1995 and continues to this day. The pre-Ron Dennis McLaren era produced two champions, Emerson Fittipaldi and James Hunt, both at the wheel of the most prevalent chassis-type ever built, the McLaren M23. With his Senna-like yellow helmet, does Lewis Hamilton consider 35 McLaren victories his minimum target? Regardless, with their keen sense of F1 history, both were aware that the first McLaren winner was a Kiwi named Bruce.

RACE VICTORIES

1. AYRTON SENNA — **35**
1988: 8 (World Champion); 1989: 6; 1990: 6 (World Champion);
1991: 7 (World Champion); 1992: 3; 1993: 5

2. ALAIN PROST — **30**
1984: 7; 1985: 5 (World Champion); 1986: 4 (World Champion);
1987: 3; 1988: 7; 1989: 4 (World Champion)

3. MIKA HÄKKINEN — **20**
1997: 1; 1998: 8 (World Champion); 1999: 5 (World Champion);
2000: 4; 2001: 2

4. DAVID COULTHARD — **12**
1997: 2; 1998: 1; 1999: 2; 2000: 3; 2001: 2; 2002: 1; 2003: 1

5. JAMES HUNT — **9**
1976: 6 (World Champion); 1977: 3

6. KIMI RÄIKKÖNEN — **9**
2003: 1; 2004: 1; 2005: 7

7. NIKI LAUDA — **8**
1982: 2; 1984: 5 (World Champion); 1985: 1

8. LEWIS HAMILTON — **8**
2007: 4; 2008: 4 to date

9. DENNY HULME — **6**
1968: 2; 1969: 1; 1972: 1; 1973: 1; 1974: 1

10. EMERSON FITTIPALDI — **5**
1974: 3 (World Champion); 1975: 2

DRIVERS WHO WON FOR WILLIAMS

Frank Williams became a GP entrant in 1969 with a Brabham for close friend Piers Courage. It was ten years of often painful endeavour before Clay Regazzoni won the first race for Williams Grand Prix Engineering, now a fully-fledged F1 constructor. With a Patrick Head designed chassis, Williams was finally a force in F1, and championships followed for Jones and Rosberg. Recognising that turbo power was the future, Williams partnered with Honda, bringing a championship to Piquet. With Honda gone, Williams sought a deal with Renault, while Head and brilliant aerodynamicist Adrian Newey pursued a design strategy which led to a six-year spell of ascendancy for Williams. World Championships for four different drivers – 1992 and 1993 Mansell and Prost, 1996 and 1997 Damon Hill and Jacques Villeneuve – is testament to the car superiority Williams enjoyed over that period, and for which their drivers must be eternally grateful. The post-Renault relationship with BMW was comparatively disappointing and Williams F1 are now in the longest period without a victory since Clay Regazzoni broke their duck in 1979.

1.	**NIGEL MANSELL** 1985: 2; 1986: 5; 1987: 6; 1991: 5; 1992: 9 (World Champion); 1994: 1	**28**
2.	**DAMON HILL** 1993: 3; 1994: 6; 1995: 4; 1996: 8 (World Champion)	**21**
3.	**ALAN JONES** 1979: 4; 1980: 5 (World Champion); 1981: 2	**11**
4.	**JACQUES VILLENEUVE** 1996: 4; 1997: 7 (World Champion)	**11**
5.	**NELSON PIQUET** 1986: 4; 1987: 3 (World Champion)	**7**
6.	**ALAIN PROST** 1993: 7 (World Champion)	**7**
7.	**RALF SCHUMACHER** 2001: 3; 2002: 1; 2003: 2	**6**
8.	**KEKE ROSBERG** 1982: 1 (World Champion); 1983: 1; 1984: 1; 1985: 2	**5**
9.	**RICCARDO PATRESE** 1990: 1; 1991: 2; 1992: 1	**4**
10.	**JUAN PABLO MONTOYA** 2001: 1; 2003: 2; 2004: 1	**4**

DRIVERS WHO WON FOR LOTUS

It is remarkable to note that in this Top Ten, only 3 drivers are still with us. Along with momentous highs, tragedy also stalked founder Colin Chapman's team, with Clark, Rindt, and Peterson perishing at the wheel of a Lotus, along with Alan Stacey, the latter two actually during a GP race. Chapman's highly innovative yet minimalist engineering techniques seemed to produce a win or bust scenario at Lotus, with spectacular performance often offset by shattering unreliability. The marque's enormous early success was achieved by one of the great partnerships in F1 folklore, that of Chapman and Clark, with subsequent championships for Hill, Rindt, Fittipaldi, and Andretti. Innes Ireland claimed the very first Team Lotus victory in 1961, but by then Stirling Moss in Rob Walker's privately-entered model had taken four, opening the Lotus account at Monaco 1960. 27 years later it was Ayrton Senna who recorded the 79th and final Lotus victory, his three-year tenure with the team producing a brief resurgence of fortune following the premature death of Colin Chapman in 1982.

1.	**JIM CLARK** 1962: 3; 1963: 7 (World Champion); 1964: 3; 1965: 6 (World Champion); 1966: 1; 1967: 4; 1968: 1	**25**
2.	**MARIO ANDRETTI** 1976: 1; 1977: 4; 1978: 6 (World Champion)	**11**
3.	**EMERSON FITTIPALDI** 1970: 1; 1972: 5 (World Champion); 1973: 3	**9**
4.	**RONNIE PETERSON** 1973: 4; 1974: 3; 1978: 2	**9**
5.	**JOCHEN RINDT** 1969: 1; 1970: 5 (World Champion)	**6**
6.	**AYRTON SENNA** 1985: 2; 1986: 2; 1987: 2	**6**
7.	**STIRLING MOSS** 1960: 2; 1961: 2; all for R. R. C. Walker	**4**
8.	**GRAHAM HILL** 1968: 3 (World Champion); 1969: 1	**4**
9.	**ELIO DE ANGELIS** 1982: 1; 1985: 1	**2**
10.	**INNES IRELAND** 1961: 1	**1**

GUNNAR NILSSON also won once for Lotus in 1977.

MOST SIGNIFICANT TECHNICAL INNOVATIONS

This Top Ten captures those occasions in GP history when F1 performance boundaries were redefined. To rank these using anything but chronology would insult those inventive minds. The criterion adopted was to contrast and compare contemporary F1 design with the very first F1 championship winner – the 1950 Alfa Romeo 158 – then select the ten cars which pioneered the evolution in shape and dynamics. Those looking for the Tyrrell P34 six-wheeler will be disappointed; innovations subsequently banned or responding purely to regulations are excluded. This eliminates such fascinating F1 cul-de-sacs as ground-effect (diffuser apart), active-ride, and traction-control. Also, F1 engine and tyre technology are omitted, given separate treatment elsewhere. Does this Top Ten suggest that since 1990 no significant technological evolution has been made? No, take McLaren's 2005 seamless-shift gearbox. It is simply that in the competitive intensity of 21st century F1 – coupled with the inevitability of regulatory constraint – performance gains are less observable. The search has shifted from fundamentals, giving seconds, to the aggregate of tweaks and embellishments bringing nano-seconds.

1.	**MERCEDES-BENZ W196** Spaceframe construction: stiff and load-bearing chassis geometry dispensed with heavy ladder-frame structure	**1954**
2.	**BRM P25** Disc brakes: initially pioneered with a single rear unit, revolutionised braking, consigning drum-brakes to history	**1956**
3.	**COOPER T43** Rear engine: weight/aerodynamic gains gave superior handling, acceleration, braking, and fuel and tyre usage	**1957**
4.	**LOTUS 25** Monocoque chassis: stiffer, lighter, smaller, load-bearing monocoque construction quickly replaced spaceframe	**1962**
5.	**LOTUS 49** Engine as chassis member: a 'stressed' engine design improved overall rigidity with attendant suspension benefits	**1967**
6.	**BRABHAM BT26** Aerofoil wings: the concept of down-force, the opposite of aircraft 'lift', produced a massive performance gain	**1968**
7.	**LOTUS 72** Side-mounted radiators; rising-rate suspension: designed to maximise downforce yet minimise resultant drag	**1970**
8.	**McLAREN MP4** Carbon-fibre composite tub; coke bottle 'waist': Improved air flow, along with enhanced chassis rigidity and safety	**1981**
9.	**FERRARI 640** Paddle-shift gearbox: fast clutchless changes, both hands to steer, tighter cockpit for aero, all found track time	**1989**
10.	**TYRRELL 019** Raised nose: this concept, bringing far-reaching airflow benefits, revolutionised the shape of the F1 car	**1990**

MOST AESTHETICALLY PLEASING F1 CARS

When gripped with fever, F1 fever, the symptoms are familiar. One is that gut-wrenching pleasure when first eyeing the sculptured lines at a long-awaited F1 car launch – intrinsically knowing it's an absolute stunner. Beauty is in the eye of the beholder, so although the top three may not gain general approval, this Top Ten should contain the personal favourite of most. But it is important to recognise the generational factor so every attempt has been made to represent the decades. For example, the aesthetics of the contemporary F1 car are challenged twice over: a surfeit of unsightly aerodynamic appendages and the striking similarity between cars. How long would it take to identify the Ferrari if all cars were painted red? Nevertheless, the 2007 Vodafone McLaren in red and chrome did make a 21st century F1 statement which deserves recognition here. And one which underlines that F1 aesthetics addresses proportions, purposefulness – and the paint job! The Lotus 79, known as Black Beauty, would be magnificent in any colour, but in black and gold, definitely number 1. And its on-track success reaffirms that well-known F1 maxim 'If it looks right, it is right'.

1. **LOTUS 79**
Poised, graceful, svelte, Black Beauty was near perfection
1978

2. **EAGLE T1G**
The beaked nose, the paint job, even the name said elegance
1967

3. **COOPER T53**
Tailfins are back while the double bonnet stripe never went away
1960

4. **FERRARI 312T**
In *travsvaal* form, Forghieri's brainchild won GPs as well as admiring glances
1975

5. **MERCEDES-BENZ W196 STREAMLINER**
So silver, so stylish, so magnificently Mercedes
1954

6. **MASERATI 250F**
Swooping bonnet, long exhaust, wire wheels, an epitome
1954

7. **McLAREN MP4-22**
With airbox-mounted 'viking' winglets, the definitive contrast to the Maserati 250F
2007

8. **BRM P160**
A purposefully handsome beast with muscular lines, chisel nose, and fragrant livery
1971

9. **LOTUS 97T**
The in-your-face turbo era produced few graceful designs. This was the exception
1985

10. **JORDAN 191**
Attractive sweep of nose and airbox made this pretty little thing as fresh as a 7-up
1991

MOST RACES BY ENGINE MAKE

The entry which shines out from this Top Ten is Ford Cosworth, a partnership of two names which changed the face of GP racing. The first was one of the largest car manufacturers the world has seen, the other a small engineering company in Northamptonshire run by Frank Costin and Keith Duckworth, thus Cosworth. This enterprise – Ford financial muscle plus Cosworth know-how – produced the 3-litre Ford Cosworth DFV V8 engine which led directly to a period in F1 history known as the 'kit-car' era. During a 15-year span from 1968, numerous constructors (about 50) used the Ford-Cosworth as their entry ticket to Formula 1. In 1974, the engine supported 16 of the 18 teams that participated (only Ferrari and BRM excepted). For the record, these were: Lotus, Tyrrell, McLaren, March, Brabham, Shadow, Surtees, Ensign, Williams (Iso Marlboro), Hesketh, Maki, Lola, Lyncar, Token, Parnelli, and Penske (plus Amon and Trojan, which both failed to qualify). As well as Ferrari, the appearance of currently active car companies like Renault, Honda, Mercedes-Benz, and BMW is evidence of the importance of manufacturer involvement and support in F1.

1.	**FERRARI** 1950 onwards: Ferrari's use of the Lancia chassis/engine over the 1956-57 seasons is included here	**772**
2.	**FORD COSWORTH** 1963-2006: The DFV and its derivatives were from 1967-91. Involvement prior to that was unofficial	**587**
3.	**RENAULT** 1977-1986; 1989-1997; 2001 onwards: innovations included turbos in 1977 and pneumatic valves in 1989	**421**
4.	**HONDA** 1964-1968; 1983-1992; 2000 onwards: Honda's golden period was for nine seasons as engine supplier from 1993	**336**
5.	**MERCEDES-BENZ** 1954-55; 1994 onwards: After almost 40 years, Mercedes re-entered F1 by acquiring engine-builders Ilmor	**261**
6.	**BMW** 1953-1955; 1968; 1982-1987; 2000 onwards: the first turbo champion resulted from the first official foray begun in 1982	**248**
7.	**ALFA ROMEO** 1950-51; 1962-63; 1965; 1970-71; 1976-1988: Alfa's official return to F1 in the 1980s showed occasional promise	**222**
8.	**BRM** 1951; 1956-1960; 1962-1977: Despite considerable success, BRM is forever associated with V16 and H16 misery	**189**
9.	**MUGEN HONDA** 1992-2000: The founder's son, Hirotoshi Honda, independently kept the flag flying during the 90s withdrawal	**147**
10.	**HART** 1981-1986; 1993-1997: Brian Hart also designed the 1998-99 Arrows engine, the first integral British car since BRM	**128**

MOST RACE WINS BY ENGINE MAKE

The foundation of any good car is a good engine. Commendatore Enzo Ferrari prided himself on manufacturing his racing engines in-house, treating anything less than engine self-sufficiency with disdain, which is ironic today given their supply to Toro Rosso and Force India. But, Ferrari aside, this Top Ten of engine wins demonstrates that manufacturers have had far more success in the role of engine supplier than when operating their own teams. With 33 team victories in their own right, Renault is followed at some distance by Alfa Romeo (10) and Mercedes-Benz (9), with Honda only 3 and BMW just 1 as a separate entity. The outsourcing of engine supply may be traced to the very origins of F1 but first came into its own with Coventry-Climax in the late 1950s, finding considerable success first with Cooper and later Lotus. Using TAG finance, McLaren made a highly successful and exclusive outsourcing deal with Porsche in the 1980s, but with 155 victories attributable to the same essential design, the Ford Cosworth DFV stands as the greatest F1 engine of all time, completing a clean sweep of victories in 1969 and 1973 in the back of respectively four and three winning constructors.

1. **FERRARI**
Ferrari (208); Toro Rosso (1)
209

2. **FORD COSWORTH**
Lotus (47); McLaren (35); Matra (9); March (3); Brabham (15); Tyrrell (23); Williams (17); Shadow (1); Hesketh (1); Penske (1); Ligier (5); Wolf (3); Benetton (14); Jordan (1); Stewart (1)
176

3. **RENAULT**
Renault (33); Lotus (5); Williams (63); Benetton (12)
113

4. **HONDA**
Honda (3); Williams (23); Lotus (2); McLaren (44)
72

5. **MERCEDES-BENZ**
Mercedes-Benz (9); McLaren (57)
66

6. **COVENTRY CLIMAX**
Cooper (14); Lotus (24); Brabham (2)
40

7. **PORSCHE**
Porsche (1); McLaren [TAG] (25)
26

8. **BMW**
Brabham (8); Benetton (1) Williams (10); BMW (1)
20

9. **BRM**
BRM (17); Lotus (1); while awaiting their highly successful V8, BRM raced one season, 1961, using Coventry-Climax engines
18

10. **ALFA ROMEO**
Alfa Romeo (10); Brabham (2)
12

5.14

MOST POWERFUL FERRARI ENGINES

A powerful and reliable motor lies at the heart of numerous Grand Prix victories. With mediocrity in the horsepower department success has been rare, although maximum power is not everything. The delivery of that power, enabling the driver to balance the car and optimise his own skills, is of no less importance. This Top Ten ranks the bhp developed by Ferrari engines over its unprecedented 59-year GP participation. Despite numerous changes in the swept volume and configuration of the motors, provoked in the main by regulatory requirements, the power curve has moved inexorably upwards from a mere 73bhp/litre in 1950 to in excess of 300bhp/litre today. Every attempt by the FIA to restrain power has resulted in an assiduous year-by-year advance as the designers and engineers find the next series of improvements. By way of example, there have been two separate periods for 3-litre engines in Formula 1. At the end of the first, in 1980, the Ferrari 'boxer' engine generated 515bhp. By the end of the second 3-litre phase in 2005, its V10 had reached 915bhp. A simple linear projection indicates an annual increment of 16bhp, or 3 per cent per annum over 25 years!

		BHP
1.	**1987** 1.5-litre 120° V6, turbocharged, longitudinally rear-mounted engine. Designer Mauro Forghieri	**1,000+**
2.	**2005** 3.0-litre 90° V10, naturally-aspirated, longitudinally rear-mounted engine. Designer Paulo Martinelli	**915**
3.	**1994** 3.5-litre 65° V12, naturally-aspirated, longitudinally rear-mounted engine. Designer Claudio Lombardi	**800**
4.	**2008** 2.4-litre 90° V8, naturally-aspirated, longitudinally rear-mounted engine. Designer Paulo Martinelli	**750**
5.	**1980** 3.0-litre 180° Flat 12 (boxer), naturally-aspirated, longitudinally rear-mounted engine. Designer Mauro Forghieri	**510**
6.	**1969** 3.0-litre 60° V12, naturally-aspirated, longitudinally rear-mounted engine. Designer Gioachino Colombo	**430**
7.	**1951** 4.5-litre 60° V12, naturally-aspirated, longitudinally front-mounted engine. Designer Aurelio Lampredi	**390**
8.	**1960** 2.5-litre 65° V6, naturally-aspirated, longitudinally front-mounted engine. Designer Vittorio Jano	**295**
9.	**1957** 2.5-litre 90° V8, naturally-aspirated, longitudinally front-mounted engine. Designer Vittorio Jano	**290**
10.	**1954** 2.5-litre in-line, 4-cylinder, naturally-aspirated, longitudinally front-mounted engine. Designer Aurelio Lampredi	**260**

MOST SUCCESSFUL ENGINE CONFIGURATION

Some 61 engine 'makes' have been brought to the Grand Prix start-line, from the diminutive (1.1-litre V-twin JAP) to the vast (4.5-litre Ferrari V12); from the simple (four-cylinder Coventry-Climax FPF) to the complex (V16 BRM); from the obscure (H16 BRM) to the bizarre (Pratt & Whitney gas-turbine), all sizes, types, and configurations seem to have been tried at one time or another (although the Life W12 never made the grid). The recent FIA decision to mandate the use of 2.4-litre V8s, now capped at 19,000rpm, suggests that the golden age of perfecting and honing the F1 internal combustion engine, which lasted more than half a century, is finally over. This means that the V8 will forever epitomise the optimal (or at least the most successful) engine configuration, having caught and passed the seemingly ubiquitous V10 since the FIA's 'V8s only' regulation. The V6 weighs in a strong third, having been the preferred configuration during the turbo era, but the surprise is that the 12-cylinder format, in either V or 'boxer' configuration – perhaps the most charismatic of the multi-cylinder engine designs because of the Ferrari connotation – finishes some way down the list.

1. **V8**
First victory: 1956 Argentine GP (Lancia Ferrari); Latest victory: 2008 Italian GP (Toro Rosso-Ferrari)
274

2. **V10**
First victory: 1989 San Marino GP (McLaren-Honda); Last victory: 2005 Chinese GP (Renault)
240

3. **V6**
First victory: 1958 French GP (Ferrari); Last victory: 1988 Australian GP (McLaren-Honda turbo)
112

4. **STRAIGHT 4**
First victory: 1952 Swiss GP (Ferrari); Last victory: 1961 US GP (Lotus-Climax)
54

5. **V12**
First victory: 1951 British GP (Ferrari); Last victory: 1995 Canadian GP (Ferrari)
41

6. **FLAT 12**
First victory: 1970 Austrian GP (Ferrari); Last victory: 1979 US GP (Ferrari)
37

7. **STRAIGHT 8**
First victory: 1950 British GP (Alfa Romeo); Last victory: 1955 Italian GP (Mercedes-Benz)
19

8. **STRAIGHT 6**
First victory: 1953 Italian GP (Maserati); Last victory: 1957 German GP (Maserati)
9

9. **FLAT 8**
Only victory: 1962 French GP (Porsche)
1

10. **H16**
Only victory: 1966 US GP (Lotus-BRM)
1

MOST SUCCESSFUL TYRE MANUFACTURERS

In the 1950s and early 1960s, despite some valuable technology transference from Firestone via the Lotus foray to Indianapolis, racing tyre development was slow. Competition sped up the process from 1966 when 'tyre wars' were waged between Goodyear, Firestone, and Dunlop. Then, in 1968, F1 cars sprouted wings. Tyre designers now worked to maximise the downforce-enhanced grip under acceleration, braking and cornering – sticky 'slicks' dispensing with treads altogether between 1971 and 1998. Michelin came and went twice, initially partnering Renault in their 1977 incursion into Grand Prix racing, and with it pioneering radial tyre construction. The withdrawal of Dunlop, then Firestone, by 1974 left US tyre giant Goodyear to make an unequalled commitment to Grand Prix racing over a period of more than three decades. The gap left by Goodyear's strategic withdrawal after 1998 was filled by Japanese tyre company Bridgestone, who have recently become the first FIA-appointed sole supplier of the F1 'control tyre'. The belief is that removal of the competitive element for F1 tyres will heighten 'the show' but lower the costs. So, no more tyre wars.

1.	**GOODYEAR** First victory: 1965 Mexican GP; Last victory: 1998 Italian GP	**368**
2.	**BRIDGESTONE** First victory: 1998 Australian GP; Last victory: Exclusive tyre supplier to F1 from 2007	**135**
3.	**MICHELIN** First victory: 1978 Brazilian GP; Last victory: 2006 Japanese GP; (withdrew between 1985 and 2000)	**102**
4.	**DUNLOP** First victory: 1958 Monaco GP; Last victory: 1970 Spanish GP	**83**
5.	**PIRELLI** First victory: 1950 British GP; Last victory: 1991 Canadian GP; (Between 1958 and 1984 Pirelli participated sporadically without success)	**45**
6.	**FIRESTONE** First victory: 1966 US GP; Last victory: 1972 Italian GP	**38**
7.	**CONTINENTAL** First victory: 1955 Argentine GP; Last victory: 1958 Argentine GP	**10**
8.	**ENGLEBERT** First victory: 1952 German GP; Last victory: 1958 British GP	**7**
9.		
10.		

Avon occasionally supplied F1 tyres, notably in the late 50s and the early 80s but were not victorious

Chapter

6

RACES AND COUNTRIES

Whether it's your national football team at the World Cup, or gold medals at the Olympic Games, everyone enjoys a touch of patriotism; it's simple human nature, a sense of belonging. Grand Prix racing is no different. The ritual raising of flags and playing of national anthems at the podium ceremony is intended to accentuate nationalism. So, despite the multinational composition of team personnel, which along with sponsorship has perhaps made Grand Prix a little less partial these days, Chapter 6 unabashedly accentuates *la différence*. As for races, 'fewest', 'most', and 'closest' are typical of the adjectives needed to describe some of the great events which will forever form part of Grand Prix posterity.

MOST GP CIRCUITS USED IN A COUNTRY

That the USA heads this table is reflective of two factors: first a certain lack of permanency for the event, and second, that at one time the following for F1 in the United States was enough to support two, and once three, races in a season. Only a visibly US-owned and operated team, or more particularly a successful American GP pilot, can ever again rekindle that level of interest. That the French GP has never found a permanent home is more intriguing but it can be traced to land mass, regionality and a cornucopia of circuits. Spain, at number three, joined the GP calendar as early as 1951, the second year of the World Championship, but it is only since the start of the 21st century, with the rise of their beloved Fernando Alonso, that F1 fever has gripped Iberia. With Valencia joining the 2008 GP schedule, the addition of this second race, making a sixth Spanish circuit venue, reaffirms the impact a successful home-grown driver can make, as does the conspicuous absence of a US GP.

1.	**UNITED STATES** Sebring (1), Riverside (1), Watkins Glen (20), Long Beach (8), Las Vegas (2), Detroit (7), Dallas (1), Phoenix (3), Indianapolis (9)	**9**
2.	**FRANCE** Reims (11), Rouen (5), Clermont-Ferrand (4), Bugatti au Mans (1), Paul Ricard (14), Dijon (6), Magny-Cours (18)	**7**
3.	**SPAIN** Pedralbes (2), Jarama (9), Montjuïc (4), Jerez (7), Catalunya (18), Valencia (1)	**6**
4.	**GREAT BRITAIN** Silverstone (42), Aintree (5), Brands Hatch (14), Donington (1)	**4**
5.	**BELGIUM** Spa-Francorchamps (41), Nivelles (2), Zolder (10)	**3**
6.	**ITALY** Monza (58), Pescara (1), Imola (26)	**3**
7.	**GERMANY** Nürburgring (37), The AVUS (1), Hockenheim (31)	**3**
8.	**PORTUGAL** Oporto (2), Monsanto Park (1), Estoril (13)	**3**
9.	**CANADA** Mosport Park (8), St Jovite (2), Montreal (30)	**3**
10.	**JAPAN** Fuji (3), Suzuka (20), Aida (2)	**3**

CLOSEST RACE FINISHES

Along with an eyeball-popping pole position lap; the cacophony of a grid start; the frenetic opening lap and a heart-stopping on-track overtake, one other constituent of the Grand Prix race which makes the blood pump faster is a frantically close finish. In the split-second world that is Grand Prix, close doesn't become electrifying until it is down to 0.1sec – around one car-length on a typical circuit. Anything less and the cars are overlapping as they take the chequered flag. Regrettably, as this Top Ten of closest GP finishes reveals, there have been precious few. Of towards 800 races since the World Championship began, there are just seven with finishes of 0.1sec or less. This table contains some wonderful Grand Prix moments, but to the shame of those involved, there are some cuckoos in the nest, three painted Ferrari rosso. Thankfully, at number one is a genuine motor race – that final Monza 'slipstreamer' when five cars crossed the line within 0.61sec, Peter Gethin's BRM winning by a couple of feet (about 70cm)! Numbers 3, 4, 5, and 7 are also authentic, but the remainder were contrived, although at number 10 the result will forever be in question – even by the winner!

1. **MONZA 1971**
Gethin edges out gang of four — **0.010**

2. **INDIANAPOLIS 2002**
Barrichello beats Schumacher in staged dead-heat — **0.011**

3. **JEREZ 1986**
Senna holds off Mansell's late charge — **0.014**

4. **ÖSTERREICHRING 1982**
de Angelis holds nerve and racing line to deny Rosberg — **0.050**

5. **MONZA 1969**
Four-car slip-streamer to Stewart — **0.080**

6. **REIMS 1954**
Formation finish by Fangio and Kling's Silver Arrows — **0.100**

7. **REIMS 1961**
Debutant Baghetti beats Porsche pair — **0.100**

8. **MONTREAL 2000**
Schumacher wins as Barrichello obeys team orders — **0.174**

9. **A1-RING 2002**
Schumacher accepts undeserved win from teammate Barrichello — **0.182**

10. **AINTREE 1955**
Fangio donates deserved home win to teammate Moss – or did he? — **0.200**

MOST VICTORIES BY NATIONALITY – DRIVERS

From Hawthorn to Hamilton, Great Britain (or more accurately the UK) has been blessed with an abundance of Grand Prix winners and World Champions. This includes three – Clark, Moss, and Stewart – who, along with just a tiny handful of other nationalities, vie in the rarefied atmosphere of the all-time greats. Brazil is another which has spawned three exceptional talents in Senna, Fittipaldi, and Piquet, whereas the three giants of mainland Europe have only each produced one true great: Schumacher (Germany), Prost (France), and Ascari (Italy). All of which makes the tiny countries of Austria (Lauda and Rindt) and Finland (Häkkinen and Räikkönen) appear to be true phenomena. Regionally, in addition to the Boys from Brazil, Latin America is represented strongly by Argentina (notably Fangio). But, after such a promising start, the greatest disappointment is the United States – ranked tenth on the list. As their love affair with NASCAR has blossomed, there has been a decline in American born or bred Grand Prix drivers. The status today is zilch, as is the case for US F1 teams and US F1 races! Thirty years have passed since Mario Andretti last scored a Grand Prix victory in the name of Uncle Sam.

1. **GREAT BRITAIN** **199**
Hawthorn (3), Moss (16), Collins (3), Brooks (6), Ireland (1), G. Hill (14), Clark (25), Surtees (6), Stewart (27), Gethin (1), Hunt (10), Watson (5), Mansell (31), D. Hill (22), Coulthard (13), Irvine (4), Herbert (3), Button (1), Hamilton (8)

2. **GERMANY** **104**
Von Trips (2), Mass (1), M. Schumacher (91), Frentzen (3), R. Schumacher (6), Vettel (1)

3. **BRAZIL** **98**
E. Fittipaldi (14), Pace (1), N. Piquet (23), Senna (41), Barrichello (9), Massa (10)

4. **FRANCE** **79**
Trintignant (2), Cevert (1), Beltoise (1), Laffite (6), Depailler (2), Jabouille (2), Prost (51), Arnoux (7), Pironi (3), Tambay (2), Alesi (1), Panis (1)

5. **ITALY** **43**
Farina (5), Fagioli (1), Ascari (13), Taruffi (1), Musso (1), Baghetti (1), Bandini (1), Scarfiotti (1), Brambilla (1), Patrese (6), de Angelis (2), Alboreto (5), Nannini (1), Fisichella (3), Trulli (1)

6. **FINLAND** **43**
Rosberg (5), Häkkinen (20), Räikkönen (17), Kovalainen (1)

7. **AUSTRIA** **41**
Rindt (6), Lauda (25), Berger (10)

8. **ARGENTINA** **38**
Fangio (24), Gonzáles (2), Reutemann (12)

9. **AUSTRALIA** **26**
Brabham (14), Jones (12)

10. **USA** **22**
P. Hill (3), Gurney (4), Ginther (1), M. Andretti (12), Revson (2)

MOST SINGLE-NATIONALITY PODIUMS

This table demonstrates the prominence of Italian drivers (and teams) in the early years of the championship and the swing in the balance of power towards Great Britain as the fifties became the sixties. The dominant teams of the early 1950s – Alfa Romeo, Ferrari, and Maserati – inevitably attracted or preferred indigenous drivers, so an 'Italian' podium was not unusual. British drivers broke through as winners sooner than British cars, and by 1958 British monikers such as Hawthorn, Moss, Brooks, and Collins could fill a victory rostrum, and did so several times. But as the development and success of the British F1 industry gathered momentum, British teams and drivers increasingly began to assert themselves on the GP circuits of the world with Clark, Graham Hill, and Surtees to the fore, although much of the latter's success came with Ferrari. France make up this Top Ten as a direct result of quasi-government intervention. The state-owned petroleum company Elf and state-supported Regie Renault encouraged a French presence in the higher echelons of international motor sport, the initiative burgeoning into numerous French GP winners – Arnoux, Laffite, Beltoise, Depailler – but just one World Champion – Alain Prost.

1. **GREAT BRITAIN**
1958: Belgian GP – T Brooks, M Hawthorn, S. Lewis-Evans; British GP – P. Collins, M. Hawthorn, R. Salvadori; Portuguese GP – S. Moss, M. Hawthorn, S. Lewis-Evans

3

2. **GREAT BRITAIN**
1965: Dutch GP – J. Clark, J. Surtees, G. Hill; French GP – J. Clark, J. Stewart, J. Surtees; British GP – J. Clark, G. Hill, J. Surtees

3

3. **ITALY**
1952: French GP – A. Ascari, G. Farina, P. Taruffi; Dutch GP – A. Ascari, G. Farina, L. Villoresi

2

4. **GREAT BRITAIN**
1964: Dutch GP – J. Clark, J. Surtees, P. Arundell; British GP – J. Clark, G. Hill, J. Surtees

2

5. **ITALY**
1950: Italian GP – G. Farina, D. Serafini/A. Ascari, L Fagioli

1

6. **ITALY**
1951: Belgian GP – G. Farina, A. Ascari, L. Villoresi

1

7. **GREAT BRITAIN**
1963: British GP – J. Clark, J. Surtees, G. Hill

1

8. **GREAT BRITAIN**
1968: United States GP – J. Stewart, G. Hill, J. Surtees

1

9. **FRANCE**
1980: Dutch GP – R. Arnoux, J. Laffite, D. Pironi

1

10. **FRANCE**
1982: French GP – R. Arnoux, A. Prost, D. Pironi

1

6.5

FEWEST CLASSIFIED FINISHERS

Small grids and poor reliability; the two factors which stalk the GP promoter's worst nightmare: as the final laps wind down, not even one car is still running to accept the chequered flag! With poor engine and gearbox reliability penalised and 18-car minimum grids 'guaranteed' by the (old) Concorde Agreement, such an outcome is unlikely these days. This Top Ten shows that the 'no classified winner' scenario has not really been that close. One venue figures prominently – Monaco. This is partly because the number of starters at Monte Carlo was invariably capped, and partly because it is a race of attrition, a renowned car breaker or driver destroyer. Even Ayrton Senna, six-time winner at the street circuit, leading the 1989 race with just 12 laps remaining, lost the 100 per cent concentration required and stuffed his McLaren into the Armco. As for worst nightmares, the organisers of the 1956 German Grand Prix at the 14-mile Nürburgring circuit must have been close to apoplexy. With a lap taking close on ten minutes, the spectators must have had to endure long periods of silent inactivity on track during a race lasting over three-and-a-half hours!

1.

1966 MONACO GP
1st J. Stewart (BRM); 2nd L. Bandini (Ferrari); 3rd G. Hill (BRM);
4th R. Bondurant (BRM)

4

2.

1996 MONACO GP
1st O. Panis (Ligier); 2nd D. Coulthard (McLaren); 3rd J. Herbert (Sauber);
4th H-H. Frentzen (Sauber)

4

3.

1956 GERMAN GP
1st J. M. Fangio (Ferrari); 2nd S. Moss (Maserati); 3rd J. Behra
(Maserati); 4th C. Godia (Maserati); 5th L. Rosier (Maserati)

5

4.

1958 GERMAN GP
1st I. Brooks (Vanwall); 2nd R. Salvadori (Cooper); 3rd M. Trintignant
(Cooper); 4th W. von Trips (Ferrari); 5th C. Allison (Lotus). Allison was the
last F1 car to finish, actually 10th behind cars in the concurrent F2 race.

5

5.

1966 BELGIAN GP
1st J. Surtees (Ferrari); 2nd J. Rindt (Cooper); 3rd L. Bandini (Ferrari); 4th
J. Brabham (Brabham); 5th R. Ginther (Cooper)

5

6.

1968 SPANISH GP
1st G. Hill (Lotus); 2nd D. Hulme (McLaren); 3rd B. Redman (Cooper); 4th
L. Scarfiotti (Cooper); 5th J.-P. Beltoise (Matra)

5

7.

1968 MONACO GP
1st G. Hill (Lotus); 2nd R. Attwood (BRM); 3rd L. Bianchi (Cooper);
4th L. Scarfiotti (Cooper); 5th D. Hulme (McLaren)

5

8.

1970 SPANISH
1st J. Stewart (March); 2nd B. McLaren (McLaren); 3rd M. Andretti
(March); 4th G. Hill (Lotus); 5th J. Servoz-Gavin (March)

5

9.

1982 SAN MARINO GP
1st D. Pironi (Ferrari); 2nd G. Villeneuve (Ferrari); 3rd M. Alboreto
(Tyrrell); 4th J.-P. Jarier (Osella); 5th E. Salazar (ATS)

5

10.

1984 DETROIT GP
1st N. Piquet (Brabham); 2nd E. de Angelis (Lotus); 3rd T. Fabi (Brabham);
4th A. Prost (McLaren); 5th J. Laffite (Williams)

5

6.6

MOST LEADERS IN A RACE

The term 'race leader' applies to the car and driver officially recorded as leading on completion of each lap and therefore ignores any other leader or lead change at any other point of the circuit during that lap. Likewise, one lap in the lead is enough to register as a race leader. The average number of race leaders has hardly changed over the decades, averaging two or three per race with very few exceptions. In fact, only 13 races have been run involving more than five leaders, and as the Top Ten table reveals, the highest number of leaders during a single Grand Prix race is eight in 1971. Most noteworthy is that one particular track features on numerous occasions: Monza. The explanation for this, as well as the presence of tracks such as Reims, the AVUS, and Hockenheim, is that these were high-speed circuits with long straights which lent themselves to the technique known as slipstreaming, where a following car can pick up a tow from the slipstream of the car ahead. This driving technique pretty much disappeared as Monza and other tracks were emasculated by chicanes in the early 1970s, a change forced upon them for reasons of safety.

1. 1971 ITALIAN GP
Monza: C. Regazzoni (Ferrari); R. Peterson (March); J. Stewart (Tyrrell); F. Cevert (Tyrrell); M. Hailwood (Surtees); J. Siffert (BRM); C. Amon (Matra); P. Gethin (BRM)

8

2. 1973 CANADIAN GP
Mosport Park: R. Peterson (Lotus); N. Lauda (BRM); E. Fittipaldi (Lotus); J. Stewart (Tyrrell); J.-P. Beltoise (BRM); J. Oliver (Shadow); P. Revson (McLaren)

7

3. 1975 BRITISH GP
Silverstone: C. Pace (Brabham); C. Regazzoni (Ferrari); T. Pryce (Shadow); J. Scheckter (Tyrrell); J.-P. Jarier (Shadow); J. Hunt (Hesketh); E. Fittipaldi (McLaren)

7

4. 1961 FRENCH GP
Reims: P. Hill (Ferrari); W. von Trips (Ferrari); R. Ginther (Ferrari); G. Baghetti (Ferrari); J. Bonnier (Porsche); D. Gurney (Porsche)

6

5. 1966 ITALIAN GP
Monza: L. Bandini (Ferrari); M. Parkes (Ferrari); J. Surtees (Cooper); J. Brabham (Brabham); D. Hulme (Brabham); L. Scarfiotti (Ferrari)

6

6. 1967 ITALIAN GP
Monza: D. Gurney (Eagle); J. Clark (Lotus); D. Hulme (Brabham); J. Brabham (Brabham); G. Hill (Lotus); J. Surtees (Honda)

6

7. 1970 ITALIAN GP
Monza: J. Ickx (Ferrari); P. Rodriguez (BRM); J. Stewart (March); C. Regazzoni (Ferrari); J. Oliver (BRM); D. Hulme (McLaren)

6

8. 1975 SPANISH GP
Montjuïc: J. Hunt (Hesketh); M. Andretti (Parnelli); R. Stommelen (Hill); C. Pace (Brabham); J. Mass (McLaren); J. Ickx (Lotus)

6

9. 1990 FRENCH GP
Paul Ricard: G. Berger (McLaren); A. Senna (McLaren); N. Mansell (Ferrari); R. Patrese (Williams); I. Capelli (Leyton House); A. Prost (Ferrari)

6

10. 1995 ITALIAN GP
Monza: D. Coulthard (Williams); G. Berger (Ferrari); J. Alesi (Ferrari); R. Barrichello (Jordan); M. Häkkinen (McLaren); J. Herbert (Benetton)

6

There were also six race leaders at the 2003 US GP, the 2004 Belgian GP, and the 2005 Japanese GP.

MOST LEAD CHANGES IN A RACE

This Top Ten of lead changes is also explained by the phenomenon of slip-streaming. The theory is that the lead car does all the work of punching a hole in the air, allowing a closely following car to be towed along in the 'slipstream' at the same speed for less work, saving some engine power and revs. The following driver then ducks out and uses these residual revs to make a pass. Slipstreaming races were invariably exciting events for spectators, involving as many as eight cars 'dicing' together for the lead. This 'dicing' ingredient explains the popularity of MotoGP, but to expect something similar from F1 racing is unrealistic. The development of F1 aerodynamics and brake and tyre technology since the late 1960s, with the correspondingly massive increase in cornering and braking power, put Grand Prix racing on an evolutionary path which can never emulate the form of racing seen in MotoGP, which is much more akin to 1950s F1. This applies to track performance too, the bike being far inferior to the car. Even Valentino Rossi would be lapped at least five times by a Formula 1 car during the course of a typical 45-minute MotoGP race.

1.
1965 ITALIAN GP
Monza: J. Clark (Lotus); G. Hill (BRM); J. Stewart (BRM)
41

2.
1970 ITALIAN GP
Monza: J. Ickx (Ferrari); P. Rodriguez (BRM); J. Stewart (March);
C. Regazzoni (Ferrari); J. Oliver (BRM); D. Hulme (McLaren)
28

3.
1964 ITALIAN GP
Monza: D. Gurney (Brabham); J. Surtees (Ferrari)
27

4.
1963 ITALIAN GP
Monza: G. Hill (BRM); J. Surtees (Ferrari); J. Clark (Lotus); D. Gurney
(Brabham)
25

5.
1971 ITALIAN GP
Monza: C. Regazzoni (Ferrari); R. Peterson (March); J. Stewart (Tyrrell);
F. Cevert (Tyrrell); M. Hailwood (Surtees); J. Siffert (BRM);
C. Amon (Matra); P. Gethin (BRM)
25

6.
1953 ITALIAN GP
Monza: A. Ascari (Ferrari); J. M. Fangio (Maserati); N. Farina (Ferrari)
24

7.
1959 GERMAN GP
The AVUS: T. Brooks (Ferrari); M. Gregory (Cooper); D. Gurney (Ferrari) ;
P. Hill (Ferrari)
24

8.
1968 ITALIAN GP
Monza: B. McLaren (McLaren); J. Surtees (Honda); J. Stewart (Matra);
J. Siffert (Lotus); D. Hulme (McLaren)
15

9.
1961 BELGIAN GP
Spa-Francorchamps: P. Hill (Ferrari); O. Gendebien (Ferrari);
W. von Trips (Ferrari)
14

10.
1969 ITALIAN GP
Monza: J. Stewart (Matra); J. Rindt (Lotus); D. Hulme (McLaren);
P. Courage (Brabham)
14

MOST RACED CIRCUITS

It seems inconceivable that Monza could ever be dropped from the Grand Prix calendar, but in 2006 complaints by local residents over noise almost achieved the impossible. Neighbours taking legal action against something that has been in situ since 1922 is surely only possible in the politically correct age in which we live. However, no circuit is free from the possibility of exclusion, as with Silverstone. As more new nations come on stream, some of the races in the European heartland of Grand Prix racing may have to go to the wall. If a European circuit cull does happen, it is hoped that the powers that be will have an eye to the rich heritage of Grand Prix racing. Five races – Britain, Monaco, Belgium, France, and Italy – and four circuits – Silverstone (first used in 1948), Monaco (1929), Spa (1924), and Monza (1922) – were on the calendar right at the start back in 1950. Of the circuits, the 'neue' Nürburgring is perhaps least evocative of its illustrious predecessor, yet somehow the Burg Nürburg landmark provides an ever-present reminder of the majesty of the Nordschleife (1927). And one of these five heritage circuits, Silverstone, hosted the very first World Championship race.

1.	**MONZA** Has staged every Italian GP except 1980 (Imola)	**58**
2.	**MONTE-CARLO** Run every year except 1951-54	**55**
3.	**SILVERSTONE** Hosted the very first World Championship race	**42**
4.	**SPA-FRANCORCHAMPS** 18 of these were held on the original long circuit	**41**
5.	**NÜRBURGRING** 22 of these were held on the Nordschleife circuit	**37**
6.	**ZANDVOORT** Home of the Dutch GP until 1985	**30**
7.	**MONTREAL** The Canadian GP has found a permanent home	**30**
8.	**IMOLA** The Autodromo Enzo e Dino Ferrari lies close to Bologna	**26**
9.	**ÖSTERREICHRING/A1-RING** 18 of these were held on the original long circuit	**25**
10.	**INTERLAGOS** The Autodromo José Carlos Pace is situated near São Paulo	**24**

MOST VICTORIES BY NATIONALITY – CARS

Rule Britannia! Classifying a team by nationality is potentially complex – ownership, location and/or team principal being the most apt identifiers. For two teams, Brabham and McLaren, there was a significant mid-term change of ownership/nationality. Both teams have always been UK-based, so a 'spiritual' approach has been taken whereby Ecclestone wins go to GB, and victories under Brabham/Tauranac are Australia. Similarly GB gain from Dennis-era McLaren success, but New Zealand is the spiritual beneficiary prior to that, regardless of Teddy Mayer's US citizenship. The lads at Enstone may also take issue that Benetton is categorised as Italian and all Renault victories go to France. Of the near 800 championship F1 races staged since 1950, 512 have been won by UK-based teams, reaffirming Britain's world-leading pre-eminence in the high-tech F1 industry. Engine manufacturers, notably from France, Japan, and Germany, who contributed massively to the success of some of the UK teams, may be placated by a similar table for F1 engines which may be found elsewhere.

1. **GREAT BRITAIN**
Vanwall (9), Cooper (16), BRM (17), Lotus (79), Brabham (22), McLaren (137), March (3), Tyrrell (23), Williams (113), Hesketh (1), Stewart (1)
421

2. **ITALY**
Alfa Romeo (10), Ferrari (208), Maserati (9), Benetton (27), Toro Rosso (1)
255

3. **FRANCE**
Matra (9), Ligier (9), Renault (33)
51

4. **NEW ZEALAND**
McLaren (24)
24

5. **AUSTRALIA**
Brabham (13)
13

6. **GERMANY**
Mercedes-Benz (9), Porsche (1), BMW (1)
11

7. **IRELAND**
Jordan (4)
4

8. **USA**
Eagle (1), Penske (1), Shadow (1)
3

9. **CANADA**
Wolf (3)
3

10. **JAPAN**
Honda (3)
3

6.10

ONLY LED THE FINAL LAP

There are few better finishes than Kimi Räikkönen's breathtaking chase from 17th grid-slot to snatch victory on the very last lap of the 2005 Japanese GP. So why doesn't it appear in this Top Ten of last lap lead changes? Because, unlike Räikkönen – whose strategy briefly gave him an earlier lead – these ten are the only GP winners to lead the final lap alone. Inevitably misfortune rather than the boldness of the eventual winner plays its part; dry fuel tanks the most common cause. But the top three were especially sensational racing finishes, engraved in F1 folklore, the most thrilling being Jochen Rindt's pursuit of Jack Brabham at Monaco in 1970. During those closing laps, as Rindt began to scent an improbable victory, he literally danced his Lotus round the classic street circuit, his final lap 0.8sec faster than pole position – and 2.7sec quicker than his own grid time! Little wonder he pressurised the great Australian into an error at the final corner, before sweeping past to a famous victory. The enduring last-lap hard-luck story must be Nigel Mansell's 1991 Canadian debacle, the only driver to lead every lap of a race – except the final one!

1. **JOCHEN RINDT**
Lotus – 1970 Monaco GP, Monte Carlo: Rindt forces Brabham error at Gasworks hairpin

10

2. **JOHN SURTEES**
Honda – 1967 Italian GP, Monza: Surtees out-drags crossed-up Brabham out of Parabolica

8

3. **RONNIE PETERSON**
Lotus – 1978 South African GP, Kyalami: Peterson forces past Depailler's ailing Tyrrell

7

4. **MARIO ANDRETTI**
Lotus – 1977 French GP, Dijon: Andretti just pips fuel-starved Watson

6

5. **BRUCE McLAREN**
Cooper – 1959 US GP, Sebring: McLaren wins while Brabham pushes it home, literally

5

6. **JIM CLARK**
Lotus – 1964 Belgian GP, Spa: McLaren's flat battery gives Clark unexpected victory

5

7. **BRUCE McLAREN**
McLaren – 1968 Belgian GP, Spa: Stewart's Matra maladies give McLaren victory

5

8. **JACQUES VILLENEUVE**
Williams – 1997 Hungarian GP, Hungaroring: Blunted Arrows leaves Damon quivering

5

9. **NELSON PIQUET**
Benetton –1991 Canadian GP, Montreal: Mansell's coasting costs consummate victory

4

10. **MIKA HÄKKINEN**
McLaren – 1997 European GP, Jerez: Villeneuve's title tendencies gift Häkkinen first win

3

In the bizarre ending to the foreshortened 2003 Brazilian GP, Giancarlo Fisichella also only led the final lap.

7

WEIRD AND WONDROUS

Just when you thought you'd seen it all, something extraordinary happens – that's the fascination of Grand Prix. As in any sport, an expectation that each and every event, game, and match will be filled with action-packed entertainment is simply wide of the mark. Similarly in F1, the racing on occasion can fall short in the thrill department, but it's a very rare GP that isn't event-filled or laced with significant overtones. This final chapter captures the more unusual and outlandish happenings that encompass Formula 1 racing: controversial or tragic, absurd or humorous, but above all, that magic F1 ingredient – the unpredictable.

SURPRISE WINNERS

As nearly 800 Grand Prix races have been run since the Drivers' World Championship began in 1950, it is extraordinary that the number of winning drivers is as few as 91. Many talented and deserving drivers never won a GP, but this Top Ten is dedicated to those with perhaps humbler expectations, who did! Prevailing circumstances, especially weather, served some well, which takes nothing from the accomplishment, although Musso and Fagioli could not have succeeded without Fangio's contribution. Some 24 years apart, two Frenchmen – Beltoise and Panis – triumphed in the wet at Monte Carlo, both winners on merit. Bonnier, Baghetti, and Scarfiotti also undoubtedly deserved their unexpected victories. In a race of attrition and tragedy, Jochen Mass found himself in the lead when the race was stopped early. But taking pride of place as the most surprising GP winner must be Vittorio Brambilla. 'The Monza Gorilla', after winning the rain-affected and foreshortened race, finally spun himself in the treacherous conditions after crossing the line, some say from the shock of being shown the chequered flag!

1. **VITTORIO BRAMBILLA**
1975 Austrian GP (March): race stopped after 29 of the scheduled 54 laps due to rain

10

2. **JOCHEN MASS**
1975 Spanish GP (McLaren): race stopped after 29 of the scheduled 75 laps following an accident killing five spectators

9

3. **LUIGI FAGIOLI**
1951 French GP (Alfa Romeo): when placed third, gave up his car to team-leader Fangio who went on to win

7

4. **LUIGI MUSSO**
1958 Argentine GP (Ferrari): when placed fifth, gave up his car to team-leader Fangio who went on to win

7

5. **ALESSANDRO NANNINI**
1989 Japanese GP (Benetton): Nannini was the beneficiary after the infamous Senna/Prost chicane shenanigans

5

6. **OLIVIER PANIS**
1996 Monaco GP (Ligier): a fine opportunist victory, with just four cars still running after two hours of racing

3

7. **JOACHIM BONNIER**
1959 Dutch GP (BRM): a BRM victory at last, and a convincing one – but it was a flash in the pan!

2

8. **LUDOVICO SCARFIOTTI**
1966 Italian GP (Ferrari): drafted in during the Surtees hiatus, Italian 'Lulu' won for Ferrari at Monza!

2

9. **GIANCARLO BAGHETTI**
1961 French GP (Ferrari): his teammates having succumbed, Ferrari's fourth driver, on debut, did the biz

1

10. **JEAN-PIERRE BELTOISE**
1972 Monaco GP (BRM): a virtuoso performance of wet-weather driving, Beltoise led every lap

1

MOTORMOUTH MURRAY

Murray Walker was not always a national treasure. Against the dulcet tones and measured delivery of a Raymond Baxter or Barry Gill, Murray's shrill and strident utterings, already familiar to viewers of televised motorbike racing, did not transfer that successfully to the F1 TV commentary box. What's more, he often perceived on-track incidents way after his audience, leaving viewers screaming at their screens in frustration. Come Monday morning, more chat surrounded Murray's howlers than the race itself. One favourite came not from F1 but Rallycross. Murray was explaining how a resourceful competitor had drilled holes in his Perspex windscreen to facilitate forward vision when the mud began flying. During his explanation, this car's screen became so totally obliterated that the unsighted driver lost control and crashed heavily. Murray was left shrieking, 'What am I saying; what am I saying!' It was James Hunt who rescued Murray as his co-commentator. James could quietly rectify the errors with, 'That's not quite right Murray!' But in the end, through strength of personality and sheer enthusiasm, Muddly Talker won the hearts of the nation.

1.	'Unless I'm very much mistaken ... I AM very much mistaken!'	**10**
2.	'Mansell is slowing it down, taking it easy. Oh, no he isn't! It's a lap record.'	**9**
3.	'There's nothing wrong with the car, except it's on fire.'	**8**
4.	'Mansell can see him in his earphone.'	**7**
5.	'Do my eyes deceive me, or is Senna's Lotus sounding rough?'	**7**
6.	'I know it's an old cliché, but you can cut the atmosphere with a cricket stump.'	**6**
7.	'You might not think that's cricket, and it's not. It's motor racing.'	**6**
8.	'Jacques Lafitte is as close to Surer as Surer is to Lafitte.'	**5**
9.	'Let's stop the startwatch.'	**5**
10.	'It's lap 26 of 58, which unless I'm very much mistaken is half way.'	**5**

Chapter Seven

RACING RELATIVES

This Top Ten reaffirms the adage that 'racing's in the blood'. A pattern has emerged in GP whereby sons are following in father's tyre-treads! As many as three of the 20-strong 2008 grid are the offspring of F1 fathers: Rosberg, Piquet, Nakajima. Whether all three have made it on merit remains to be seen. Certainly two of their predecessors, Damon Hill and Jacques Villeneuve, more than justified their presence by carrying off a world title each. With two F1 championships for father Graham and one for son Damon, the Hill dynasty must be regarded as the number one racing relatives in F1. Of the racing brothers, the Schumacher's take some beating and also hold the unique distinction of the first brotherly 1-2 finish at Montreal in 2001. Despite all the glory, relief must abound within family Schumacher that their F1 days are behind them. Fortune was less kind to the Rodriguez family. In 1962 younger brother Ricardo, aged just 20, was tragically killed in practice for his home GP in Mexico City. This made elder brother Pedro determined to take up Ricardo's fallen mantle, which he did with considerable success and verve until, in 1971, he too became a motor sport casualty.

1.	**HILL** Father and son: Graham 1962 and 1968 World Champion; Damon 1996 World Champion	**10**
2.	**VILLENEUVE** Father and son: Gilles GP-winner (6) 1978-81; Jacques 1997 World Champion	**7**
3.	**SCHUMACHER** Brothers: Michael 1994, 1995, and 2000-04 World Champion; Ralf GP-winner (6) 2001-03	**6**
4.	**BRABHAM** Father and sons: Jack 1959, 1960, and 1966 World Champion; Gary GP-entrant 1990, NPQ; David GP-driver 1990 and 1994, best result 10th	**4**
5.	**ANDRETTI** Father and son: Mario 1978 World Champion; Michael GP-driver 1993 best result 3rd	**4**
6.	**PIQUET** Father and son: Nelson 1981, 1983, and 1987 World Champion; Nelsinho GP driver 2008, best result 2nd	**4**
7.	**FITTIPALDI** Brothers: Emerson 1972 and 1974 World Champion; Wilson GP driver 1972-75, best result 5th; Christian (Wilson's son) GP driver 1992-1994, best result 4th	**3**
8.	**SCHECKTER** Brothers: Jody 1979 World Champion; Ian GP-driver 1974-77 best result 10th	**3**
9.	**STEWART** Brothers: Jackie 1969, 1971, and 1973 World Champion; Jimmy GP-driver 1953, retired from race	**2**
10.	**RODRIGUEZ** Brothers: Ricardo GP-winner (2) 1967 and 1970; Pedro GP-driver 1961-62, best result 4th	**1**

Also worthy of mention are: WHITEHEAD, Peter and Graham (half-brothers); PARNELL, Reg and Tim (father and son); BRAMBILLA, Vittorio and Ernesto (brothers), and again, VILLENEUVE, Gilles and Jacques (brothers).

BLUE RIBAND WINNERS

It is widely accepted that there are three blue riband events in motor sport, each of which presents the driver with a unique challenge: the F1 World Championship series, the Indianapolis 500-mile race on a banked 1.67 mile oval, and the Le Mans 24-hour endurance race. Before it became all-consuming, there was a time when F1 drivers participated in different forms of motor sport alongside their GP commitments. For the GP stars it was an opportunity to (usually) assert their authority in other types and levels of racing. For their challengers, it was a chance to (occasionally) put one over on the greats. Progression into F1 nowadays is far more linear, and once in situ, extra-curricular racing activities are frowned upon. Today it is not until the après-F1 period that it is possible to observe the success or otherwise of the GP pilot in other categories, whether it be DTM, IRL, ALMS or even NASCAR. His 1972 Le Mans win made Graham Hill the only driver to have been successful in all three blue riband disciplines, a feat that the great all-rounder Mario Andretti dearly wanted to emulate, and which Jacques Villeneuve is still working on!

1. **GRAHAM HILL**
F1: 1962 and 1968 World Champion; Indianapolis 500: 1966 winner; Le Mans: 1972 winner

10

2. **JIM CLARK**
F1: 1963 and 1965 World Champion; Indianapolis 500: 1965 winner; Tasman Cup: 1965 and 1967-68

8

3. **EMERSON FITTIPALDI**
F1: 1972 and 1974 World Champion; Indianapolis 500: 1989 and 1993 winner; 'Indycar' Champion: 1989

8

4. **MARIO ANDRETTI**
F1: 1970 World Champion; Indianapolis 500: 1969 winner; 'Indycar' Champion: 1965-66, 1969 and 1984

7

5. **JACQUES VILLENEUVE**
F1: 1997 World Champion; Indianapolis 500: 1995 winner; 'Indycar' Champion: 1995

7

6. **NIGEL MANSELL**
F1: 1992 World Champion; 'Indycar' Champion: 1993

6

7. **PHIL HILL**
F1: 1961 World Champion; Le Mans: 1958 and 1961-62 winner

6

8. **MIKE HAWTHORN**
F1: 1958 World Champion; Le Mans: 1955 winner

5

9. **JOCHEN RINDT**
F1: 1970 World Champion; Le Mans: 1965 winner

5

10. **JACKY ICKX**
F1: GP winner (8) 1968-72; Le Mans: 1969, 1975-77 and 1981-82 winner; Can-Am: 1979 Champion

4

7.5

HEROES TO ZEROES

Of the 29 F1 drivers to be crowned World Champion, eight successfully defended with back-to-back championships. Michael Schumacher and Juan Manuel Fangio surpassed even that with, respectively, five and four successive titles. Jochen Rindt was awarded his posthumously, and another four champions chose not to defend, taking retirement instead. This table is the ten drivers who did campaign the following season as reigning World Champion yet achieved very little, failing to win even one race – on top one year, scratching for solid results the next. The top four were never to win a GP again; for Jacques Villeneuve, a drought that would last nine long years! Damon Hill, John Surtees, and Nelson Piquet would all revisit the top step of the podium later in their careers, and Sir Jack Brabham had yet another championship title in him. In some ways it is inappropriate for Fangio to be included, bringing his illustrious career to an end during that same year. Topping the table, an invidious accolade, is Jody Scheckter. In the season following his 1979 championship, he earned just two points, and at Montreal even failed to qualify. Scheckter retired at season's end.

1. **JODY SCHECKTER**
1979: World Champion, Ferrari; 1980: 19th with 2 championship points, best result 5th, Ferrari
10

2. **JACQUES VILLENEUVE**
1997: World Champion, Williams; 1998: 5th with 21 championship points, best result 3rd, Williams
9

3. **PHIL HILL**
1961: World Champion, Ferrari; 1962: 6th with 14 championship points, best result 2nd, Ferrari
7

4. **MARIO ANDRETTI**
1978: World Champion, Lotus; 1979: 10th with 14 championship points, best result 3rd, Lotus
7

5. **JOHN SURTEES**
1964: World Champion, Ferrari; 1965: 5th with 17 championship points, best result 2nd, Ferrari
4

6. **DAMON HILL**
1996: World Champion, Williams; 1997: 12th with 7 championship points, best result 2nd, Arrows
4

7. **NELSON PIQUET**
1987: World Champion, Williams; 1988: 6th with 22 championship points, best result 3rd, Lotus
4

8. **ALBERTO ASCARI**
1953: World Champion, Ferrari; 1954: 25th with 1.14 championship points, best result Retired, Maserati, Ferrari, Lancia
1

9. **JUAN MANUEL FANGIO**
1957: World Champion, Maserati; 1958: 14th with 7 championship points, best result 4th, Maserati
1

10. **JACK BRABHAM**
1960: World Champion, Cooper; 1961: 11th with 4 championship points, best result 4th , Cooper
1

TWO WHEELS TO FOUR

Riding motorbikes is one way seven-times F1 World Champion Michael Schumacher gets his kicks since retirement. Five-times MotoGP champion Valentino Rossi regularly tested an F1 Ferrari in 2006. Just two illustrations of the narrow divide between two great motor sport disciplines, two wheels and four, a storyline given a fascinating twist by the top two, John Surtees and Mike Hailwood. Both were true biking legends when they entered F1, Surtees pivotal in reviving Ferrari's fortunes, taking them to championship glory in 1964 to gain the unique distinction of winning world titles on two wheels and on four. Later he was to campaign his own car and team for nine seasons, but without major success. After an initial foray in the 1960s, Mike 'The Bike' Hailwood returned to F1 in 1971 with Big John's eponymous team, but success eluded the pair and Hailwood moved on. A career-ending accident curtailed a highly promising 1974 season at Yardley McLaren, but Mike wasn't done yet, winning on the daunting Isle of Mann TT circuit in 1978 and 1979. Two years later Mike Hailwood MBE MC was killed in a road accident aged 41. Until recently, John Surtees OBE ran the British A1GP team.

1. **JOHN SURTEES**
Bikes: 1952-60 7-times World Champion at 350cc (3) and 500cc (4)
F1: 1960-72 111 GP starts, 6 wins, 1964 World Champion

10

2. **MIKE HAILWOOD**
Bikes: 1958-67 9-times World Champion at 250cc (3), 350cc (2) and 500cc (4). F1: 1963-65 and 1971-74 49 GP starts, 29 championship points, best result 2nd

7

3. **JOHNNY CECOTTO**
Bikes: 1975-80 2-times World Champion at 350cc (1) and Formula 750 (1)
F1: 1983-84 18 GP starts, 1 championship point, best result 6th

5

4. **PIERO TARUFFI**
Bikes: Competed in 1930s becoming 500cc European Champion in 1932
F1: 1950-52 and 1954-56 18 GP starts, 1 win, 41 championship points

4

5. **NELLO PAGANI**
Bikes: 1949-55 competed in World Championship motor cycle racing, winning 125cc title in 1949
F1: 1950 1 GP start, 0 championship points, best result 7th

3

6. **BOB ANDERSON**
Bikes: 1958-60 competed in World Championship motor cycle racing, with three podium finishes
F1: 1963-67 25 GP starts, 8 championship points, best result 3rd

3

7. **PADDY DRIVER**
Bikes: 1959-65 finishing third in the 1965 500cc World Championship
F1: 1963 and 1974 1 GP start, 0 championship points, best result Ret'd

3

8. **KUNIMITSU TAKAHASHI**
Bikes: 1960-64 competed in 125cc and 250cc World Championships, winning four GPs
F1: 1977 1 GP start, 0 championship points, best result 9th

3

9. **DAMON HILL**
Bikes: 1983-84 entered competitive motorsport, winning the 350cc Clubman's Cup at Brands Hatch
F1: 1992-99 116 GP starts, 22 wins, 1996 World Champion

2

10. **PEDRO LAMY**
Bikes: 1988 entered competitive motorsport via Motocross
F1: 1993-96 32 GP starts, 1 championship point, best result 6th

1

TEAM ORDERS OBEYED – AND IGNORED!

GP racing always was a team game. In the early days, if the team leader dropped out, the number two could be asked to hand over his healthy car. Fangio and Moss won races this way, and in probably the most selfless act in GP history, Peter Collins gave Fangio his car and with it his own chance of championship honours. Team orders typically arise when one team driver is better placed to win the championship. It was such which caused the FIA to ban the practice in 2002. Ferrari policy demanded that teammates, by contract, should not compromise Michael Schumacher's championship points position. When Rubens Barrichello dutifully gave up a highly deserved win in sight of the chequered flag, all hell broke loose. But 1982 produced a different team-orders hell. Reneging on a pre-race agreement, Didier Pironi stole a race from team-leader Gilles Villeneuve on the final lap of the San Marino GP. A principled man, Villeneuve was genuinely shocked by this deceit. At the following race Gilles perished. One can only speculate as to the extent that Villeneuve's fatal accident resulted from his general state of mind following Imola.

1. PETER COLLINS

Obeyed: Monza 1956, voluntarily handed over his car 15 laps from championship glory. **Beneficiary:** Ferrari team-leader Fangio became 1956 champion, his fourth world title

10

2. GILLES VILLENEUVE

Obeyed: Monza 1979, dutiful 1-2 finish relinquished his own championship chances. **Beneficiary:** Ferrari team-leader Scheckter became 1979 World Champion

9

3. RONNIE PETERSON

Obeyed: Zandvoort 1978, Ronnie's penultimate GP, was his fourth dutiful 1-2 finish. **Beneficiary:** Lotus team-leader Andretti became 1978 World Champion

8

4. TONY BROOKS

Obeyed: Silverstone 1957, handed over his car and shared unique glory with Moss. **Beneficiary:** Vanwall team-leader Moss's victory was the first for a British car

7

5. DAVID COULTHARD

Obeyed: Melbourne 1998, Coulthard acknowledged compromised orders, conceding Round 1. **Beneficiary:** Häkkinen led this McLaren 1-2 and never looked back, taking 1998-99 championships

6

6. RUBENS BARRICHELLO

Obeyed: A1-Ring 2002, Barrichello's infamously late donation in a Ferrari 1-2. **Beneficiary:** Ferrari team-leader Schumacher progressed towards the 2002 championship, his fifth

5

7. MICHAEL SCHUMACHER

Obeyed: Sepang 1999, out of contention through injury, Schumacher played the game. **Beneficiary:** Irvine led this Ferrari 1-2 but failed to win the 1999 championship

4

8. RENE ARNOUX

Ignored: Paul Ricard 1982, Arnoux was never going to concede this home 1-2 finish
Duped: Renault team-leader Alain Prost was none too pleased

0

9. CARLOS REUTEMANN

Ignored: Rio 1981, Carlos mades it plain as early as Round 2 that team orders were not for him. **Duped:** Reigning champion Alan Jones was not impressed to finish second in a Williams 1-2

0

10. DIDIER PIRONI

Ignored: Imola 1982, Pironi disobeyed orders in Ferrari 1-2 finish
Duped: Ferrari team-leader Gilles Villeneuve was killed at the next race

-10

7.8

CONTROVERSIAL COLLISIONS

The fundamental which separates GP racing past from GP racing present is danger. GP remains highly dangerous, but safety has improved such that deliberate car-on-car contact has been used to decide the outcome of races, even championships. Traditionally the mindset of the GP driver had to be 'win, but not at all costs' because of potentially fatal consequences. Many believe that the Prost/Senna feud which culminated in those championship-deciding collisions at Suzuka in 1989 and 1990 allowed a genie to escape from the bottle. First Senna and then Schumacher altered the unwritten rules to 'win at all costs', with the threat or actuality of an accident overt, if unspoken. From a blend of skill with nerve, Grand Prix racing had become a blend of skill and intimidation. However, car-on-car contact is not part of Formula 1 racing and never can be. Clashes between cars, where no fault can be apportioned, are deemed 'racing incidents'. But contact resulting from behaviour that is deliberate, premeditated or even threatened is deplorable. Michael Schumacher's retirement hopefully draws a line under such unacceptable conduct.

1. **SENNA-PROST**
1990 Suzuka: Senna deliberately wreaks 1989 revenge
10

2. **SCHUMACHER-D. HILL**
1994 Adelaide: Schumacher collects championship after deliberate collision
10

3. **SCHUMACHER-VILLENEUVE**
1997 Jerez: Schumacher disqualified from championship for another intentional collision
10

4. **PROST-SENNA**
1989 Suzuka: Prost inadvertently uncorks the 'collision' genie
8

5. **BANDINI-G. HILL**
1964 Mexico City: Surtees champion as Ferrari teammate Bandini runs into contender Hill
6

6. **D. HILL-SCHUMACHER**
1995 Silverstone and Monza: Damon vainly tries Schumacher-style win or bust tactics
5

7. **SENNA-BRUNDLE**
1989 Adelaide: Senna clouts Brundle in wall of spray, ending tenuous title chances
3

8. **COULTHARD-SCHUMACHER**
1998 Spa: Blinded by spray and subsequent anger, Schumacher shunts innocent Coulthard
3

9. **PIQUET-SALAZAR**
1982 Hockenheim: Piqued Piquet punches out after losing lead lapping Salazar
2

10. **SENNA-SCHLESSER**
1988 Monza: Senna trips over debutant Schlesser to deny McLaren-Honda full-house
2

BAD BOYS – BANS AND DISQUALIFICATIONS

Seven-times champion Michael Schumacher's incredible all-round driving talent is greatly admired. But has his F1 legacy been destroyed by his serial transgressions? Cheating makes sport utterly pointless. 'May the best man win' becomes 'let the best cheat get away with it'. Is there the slightest interest in the achievements of Ben Johnson, Dwayne Chambers, or Bruce Grobbelar – three self-confessed cheats who spring to mind? Setting aside Schumacher's team misdemeanours, his personal wrongdoings include: barging into Damon Hill, following his own driving error, to 'win' his first World Championship title; attempting the same stunt with Jacques Villeneuve three years later; numerous faked finishes with Rubens Barrichello; his feigned 'off' at Rascasse in 2006 Monaco qualifying; and at Interlagos in 1995 being found to weigh 5.5kg less after the race than before it, raising the suspicion that he had been carrying ballast at the pre-race weigh-in. To quote Jacques Villeneuve: 'The reason Michael Schumacher did what he did is that he thinks he is better than the rest of us. He thinks he is bigger than the sport too, but he isn't. And when he retires, and no one really remembers him, that will become clear.'

1. **MICHAEL SCHUMACHER**
Banned for ignoring black flag (1994: 2 races); disqualified from 1st place due to 'plank' wear infringement (1994: 1 race); disqualified from championship for deliberate collision (1997: 17 races)

20

2. **STEFAN BELLOF**
Team disqualifications due to technical infringement, 1984 'weight' Tyrrell

11

3. **MARTIN BRUNDLE**
Team disqualifications due to technical infringement, 1984 'weight' Tyrrell (7); 1987 'bodywork' Zakspeed (1)

8

4. **STEFAN JOHANSSON**
Team disqualifications due to technical infringement, 1984 'weight' Tyrrell (3); 1989 disqualified for ignoring black flag (1)

4

5. **EDDIE IRVINE**
Banned for dangerous driving, 1984

3

6. **JENSON BUTTON**
Team disqualifications due to technical infringement, 2005 'weight' Honda

2

7. **TAKUMA SATO**
Team disqualifications due to technical infringement, 2005 'weight' Honda

2

8. **NIGEL MANSELL**
Banned for ignoring black flag, 1989

1

9. **MIKA HÄKKINEN**
Banned for dangerous driving, 1994

1

10. **JAMES HUNT**
Disqualified from 1st place due to use of spare car at re-start, 1976

1

Also disqualified from 1st place were NELSON PIQUET in 1982 and ALAIN PROST in 1985 both due to 'weight' infringements, and AYRTON SENNA in 1989 due to an illegal push start.

Chapter Seven

7.10

SCARY STARTS
– PILE-UPS

The grid start is a stunning experience – one of GP's greatest spectacles. Twenty-plus of the world's fastest cars and drivers form up in close proximity. The five red lights blink on, the engine revs soar to a shrieking crescendo of power, the ground trembles, the air pulsates as 15,000-plus bhp is held for those long, final moments before being unleashed. Suddenly the lights are go and the cars blast away, gathering pace at an astonishing rate towards the horizon of the first corner, jinking and weaving to find a gap as they descend en masse towards turn one. Turn one is what this Top Ten is mainly about. Simultaneously releasing a group of young men in fast cars is bound periodically to end in tears. This became clear at Monaco in 1950 when ten cars were eliminated on lap one of only the second race of the entire World Championship series. Although many drivers have been injured in a first lap pile up, thankfully it has resulted only once in total catastrophe. Just one of our ten was not a scary start, sudden rain producing a scary and premature ending to the 1975 British GP in an eight-car scrap heap.

1.	**1978 ITALIAN GP** Shambolic start, calamitous consequences	**11**
2.	**1998 BELGIAN GP** Coulthard creates carnage	**11**
3.	**1950 MONACO GP** Tabac debacle on first lap	**10**
4.	**1973 BRITISH GP** Scheckter's lap 1 Woodcote mêlée	**9**
5.	**1986 BRITISH GP** Paddock Hill Bend bedlam	**9**
6.	**1975 BRITISH GP** Club Corner chaos on lap 56	**8**
7.	**1980 CANADIAN GP** Thackwell's record breaking debut!	**8**
8.	**1979 ARGENTINE GP** First corner collision causes carnage	**7**
9.	**1989 FRENCH GP** Gugelmin drops in on Mansell	**7**
10.	**1984 EUROPEAN GP** New Nürburgring circuit, old first corner problems	**6**

WORST WEEKENDS

This is not a Top Ten, simply a remembrance of the darker side of GP racing. The threat of death or serious injury once control of an F1 car is lost can never be eliminated, but that those involved in the sport can participate comparatively safely these days is testament to some outstanding work in the quest for safety. This selection largely evokes tragic images long past, but also memories of some triumphant ones when human courage and bravery transcended catastrophe, or attempted to: Arturo Merzario releasing Niki Lauda from his burning Ferrari so the great Austrian would cheat death and race another day; Mike Hailwood saving the unconscious Clay Regazzoni from his burning BRM, and most poignant of all, David Purley's repeated but unsuccessful attempts to rescue Roger Williamson from his flaming overturned wreck. Hailwood and Purley received the George Medal. In the first 32 years ending 1982, 22 drivers lost their lives during GP events. In the subsequent 26 years, the death toll is two. Despite the elimination of driver fatalities since 1994, the one great danger facing GP racing today is complacency.

19 OCTOBER 1958, CASABLANCA
Moroccan GP: Lewis-Evans is third fatality that season

19 JUNE 1960, SPA-FRANCORCHAMPS
Belgian GP: One race, two unrelated fatalities, Bristow and Stacey

10 SEPTEMBER 1961, MONZA
Italian GP: Wolfgang von Trips and 15 spectators are killed

7 MAY 1967, MONTE CARLO
Monaco GP: Bandini's Ferrari burns after striking chicane

7 JULY 1968, ROUEN-LES-ESSARTS
French GP: Debutant Schlesser dies in burning Honda

6 SEPTEMBER 1970, MONZA
Italian GP: Another double hammer-blow; first Courage, now Rindt

6 OCTOBER 1973, WATKINS GLEN
United States GP: Cevert's death came so soon after the Williamson tragedy

10 SEPTEMBER 1978, MONZA
Italian GP: Ronnie's death 24 hours later was a terrible shock

13 JUNE 1982, MONTREAL
Canadian GP: Canada endured Paletti's fatality only one month after Gilles

15 MAY 1994, MONTE CARLO
Monaco GP: Wendlinger in coma just 12 days after Mayday Imola mayhem

THE TOP TEN ALL-TIME F1 DRIVERS

A fitting conclusion is that intriguing quest for 'The Greatest'.
Fortuitously, the Haynes publication *Analysing Formula 1* recently
reopened this perennial debate. This fact-based analysis of GP
racing ranked the great drivers since 1950 using a consistent
methodology incorporating measurement imperatives such as car
superiority and competitive strength. Hard on its heels came an
opinion-based list from F1 sage Alan Henry, and finally *F1 Racing*
magazine chimed in with a reader-based survey. Of course, there
is no single answer; each source as valid or as unfounded as the
next. The one based on opinion placed Stirling Moss number one;
the one using perception gave it to Ayrton Senna, and the scientific
approach produced Juan Manuel Fangio. The most authoritative
version, as used here, is a 'poll-of-polls' averaging the three. And
the deserving winner? That sublime and greatly loved driver Jimmy
Clark. As Dan Gurney attested, 'Jimmy was a "natural".' His
sensational speed came from consistency of track placement, early
on the brakes (slow in), early on the power (fast out), coupled with
silky smoothness. He made the rest look 'agricultural'.

1. JIM CLARK
GP starts: 72; GP wins: 25; Strike rate 35%;
2 World Championships 1963 and 1965

10

2. JUAN MANUEL FANGIO
GP starts: 51; GP wins: 24; Strike rate 47%;
5 World Championships 1951 and 1954-57

9

3. AYRTON SENNA
GP starts: 161; GP wins: 41; Strike rate 25%;
3 World Championships 1988 and 1990-91

9

4. ALAIN PROST
GP starts: 199; GP wins: 51; Strike rate 26%;
4 World Championships 1985-86, 1989 and 1993

8

5. MICHAEL SCHUMACHER
GP starts: 249; GP wins: 91; Strike rate 37%;
7 World Championships 1994-95, 2000-04

7

6. STIRLING MOSS
GP starts: 66; GP wins: 16; Strike rate 24%,
0 World Championships, runner-up 1955-58

6

7. JACKIE STEWART
GP starts: 99; GP wins: 27; Strike rate 27%;
3 World Championships 1969, 1971 and 1973

6

8. MIKA HÄKKINEN
GP starts: 161; GP wins: 20; Strike rate 12%;
2 World Championships 1998-99

4

9. ALBERTO ASCARI
GP starts: 31; GP wins: 13; Strike rate 42%;
2 World Championships 1952-53

3

10. NIKI LAUDA
GP starts: 171; GP wins: 25; Strike rate 15%;
3 World Championships 1975, 1977 and 1984

3

BIBLIOGRAPHY

Magazines and annuals
Autocourse   Autosport   F1 Racing

Websites
FORIX on Autosport.com

Books

Aaron, Simon/Hughes, Mark, *The Complete Book of Formula One*,
(Motorbooks International, 2003)

Hayhoe, David and Holland, David, *Grand Prix Data Book*,
(Haynes Publishing, 2006)

Henry, Alan, *The Top 100 F1 Drivers of All Time*, (Icon Books Ltd, 2008)

—, *Williams – Formula 1 racing team*, (Haynes Publications, 1998)

Higham, Peter, *The International Motor Racing Guide*, (David Bull Publishing, 2003)

Hodges, David, *A-Z of Grand Prix Cars*, (The Crowood Press Ltd, 2001)

Hughes, Mark, *The unofficial Formula One Encyclopaedia*,
(Anness Publishing, 2004)

Lang, Mike, *Grand Prix! – Volume 1: 1950-1965*, (Haynes Publishing, 1981)

—, *Grand Prix! – Volume 2: 1966-1973*, (Haynes Publishing, 1982)

—, *Grand Prix! – Volume 3: 1974-1980*, (Haynes Publishing, 1983)

—, *Grand Prix! – Volume 4: 1981-1984*, (Haynes Publishing, 1992)

Ménard, Pierre, *The Great Encyclopaedia of Formula 1*,
(Constable & Robinson Ltd, 2000)

Mondadori, Arnoldo/Nada, Giorgio, *Ferrari – All the cars*,
(Haynes Publishing, 2005)

Noakes, Andrew, *The Ford Cosworth DFV*, (Haynes Publishing, 2007)

Nye, Doug, *Theme Lotus 1956-1986 – From Chapman to Ducarouge*,
(Motor Racing Publications, 1986)

—, *McLaren – The Grand Prix, Can-Am and Indy cars*, (Hazleton Publishing, 1988)

Raby, Philip, *Grand Prix Driver by Driver*, (Green Umbrella Publishing, 2007)

Small, Steve, *Grand Prix Who's Who*, (Travel Publishing Ltd, 2000)

Smith, Roger, *Analysing Formula 1*, (Haynes Publishing, 2008)

Tibballs, Geoff, *Motor-Racing's Strangest Races*, (Robson Books, 2001)

White, John, *Formula One Facts & Trivia*, (Carlton Books Limited, 2007)

Zapelloni, Umberto, *Formula Ferrari*, (Hodder & Stoughton, 2004)

NATIONALITIES OF LISTED DRIVERS

Argentina *(ARG)*; Australia *(AUS)*; Austria *(AUT)*; Belgium *(BEL)*; Brazil *(BRA)*; Canada *(CAN)*; Chile *(CHI)*; Columbia *(COL)*; Spain *(ESP)*; Finland *(FIN)*; France *(FRA)*; Great Britain & Northern Ireland *(GBR)*; Germany *(GER)*; Ireland *(IRL)*; Italy *(ITA)*; Japan *(JPN)*; Mexico *(MEX)*; The Netherlands *(NED)*; New Zealand *(NZL)*; Portugal *(POR)*; South Africa *(RSA)*; Switzerland *(SUI)*; Sweden *(SWE)*; United States of America *(USA)*; Venezuela *(VEN)*

Alboreto, Michele *(ITA)*
Alesi, Jean *(FRA)*
Alliot, Phillipe *(FRA)*
Allison, Cliff *(GBR)*
Alonso, Fernando *(ESP)*
Amati, Giovanna *(ITA)*
Amon, Chris *(NZL)*
Anderson, Bob *(GBR)*
Andretti, Mario *(USA)*
Andretti, Michael *(USA)*
Arnoux, Rene *(FRA)*
Arundell, Peter *(GBR)*
Ascari, Alberto *(ITA)*
Attwood, Richard *(GBR)*
Badoer, Luca *(ITA)*
Baghetti, Giancarlo *(ITA)*
Bandini, Lorenzo *(ITA)*
Barrichello, Rubens *(BRA)*
Bellof, Stefan *(GER)*
Beltoise, Jean-Pierre *(FRA)*
Behra, Jean *(FRA)*
Berger, Gerhard *(AUT)*
Bernoldi, Enrique *(BRA)*
Beuttler, Mike *(GBR)*
Bianchi, Lucien *(BEL)*
Bondurant, Bob *(USA)*

Bonnier, Jo *(SWE)*
Boutsen, Thierry *(BEL)*
Brabham, David *(AUS)*
Brabham, Gary *(AUS)*
Brabham, Jack *(AUS)*
Brambilla, Ernesto *(ITA)*
Brambilla, Vittorio *(ITA)*
Bristow, Chris *(GBR)*
Brooks, Tony *(GBR)*
Brundle, Martin *(GBR)*
Button, Jenson *(GBR)*
Capelli, Ivan *(ITA)*
Castellotti, Eugenio *(ITA)*
Cecotto, Johnny *(VEN)*
Cevert, Francoise *(FRA)*
Cheever, Eddie *(USA)*
Clark, Jim *(GBR)*
Collins, Peter *(GBR)*
Coulthard, David *(GBR)*
Courage, Piers *(GBR)*
Dalmas, Yannick *(FRA)*
Daly, Derek *(IRL)*
de Angelis, Elio *(ITA)*
de Cesaris, Andrea *(ITA)*
de Filippis, Maria-Teresa *(ITA)*

Depailler, Patrick *(FRA)*
Driver, Paddy *(RSA)*
Fabi, Teo *(ITA)*
Fagioli, Luigi *(ITA)*
Fangio, Juan Manuel *(ARG)*
Farina, Nino *(ITA)*
Fisichella, Giancarlo *(ITA)*
Fittipaldi, Emerson *(BRA)*
Fittipaldi, Wilson *(BRA)*
Frentzen, Heinz-Harald *(GER)*
Gachot, Bertrand *(FRA)*
Galica, Divina *(GBR)*
Gendebien, Olivier *(BEL)*
Gethin, Peter *(GBR)*
Ghinzani, Piercarlo *(ITA)*
Ginther, Richie *(USA)*
Godia, Francesco *(ESP)*
González, Froilan *(ARG)*
Gregory, Masten *(USA)*
Gugelmin, Mauricio *(BRA)*
Gurney, Dan *(USA)*
Hailwood, Mike *(GBR)*
Häkkinen, Mika *(FIN)*

Hamilton, Lewis (GBR)
Hawthorn, Mike (GBR)
Heidfeld, Nick (GER)
Henton, Brian (GBR)
Herbert, Johnny (GBR)
Hill, Damon (GBR)
Hill, Graham (GBR)
Hill, Phil (USA)
Hulme, Denny (NZL)
Hunt, James (GBR)
Ickx, Jacky (BEL)
Ireland, Innes (GBR)
Irvine, Eddie (GBR)
Jabouille, Jean-Pierre (FRA)
Jarier, Jean-Pierre (FRA)
Johansson, Stefan (SWE)
Jones, Alan (AUS)
Keegan, Rupert (GBR)
Kovalainen, Heikki (FIN)
Laffite, Jacques (FRA)
Lammers, Jan (NED)
Lamy, Pedro (POR)
Larini, Nicola (ITA)
Lauda, Niki (AUT)
Lewis-Evans, Stuart (GBR)
Lombardi, Lella (ITA)
Lovely, Pete (USA)
Lunger, Brett (USA)
Mansell, Nigel (GBR)
Marques, Tarso (BRA)
Martini, Pierluigi (ITA)
Mass, Jochen (GER)
Massa, Felipe (BRA)
McLaren, Bruce (NZL)
Merzario, Arturo (ITA)
Montoya, Juan Pablo
  (COL)
Moreno, Roberto
  (BRA)
Moss, Stirling (GBR)
Musso, Luigi (ITA)

Nannini, Alessandro (ITA)
Nilsson, Gunnar (SWE)
Oliver, Jackie (GBR)
Pace, Carlos (BRA)
Pagani, Nello (ITA)
Paletti, Riccardo (ITA)
Panis, Olivier (FRA)
Parkes, Mike (GBR)
Patrese, Ricardo (ITA)
Peterson, Ronnie (SWE)
Pilette, Andre (BEL)
Piquet, Nelsinho (BRA)
Piquet, Nelson (BRA)
Pironi, Didier (FRA)
Prost, Alain (FRA)
Pryce, Tom (GBR)
Räikkönen, Kimi (FIN)
Redman, Brian (GBR)
Regazzoni, Clay (SUI)
Reutemann, Carlos (ARG)
Revson, Peter (USA)
Rindt, Jochen (AUT)
Rodríguez, Pedro (MEX)
Rodríguez, Ricardo (MEX)
Rosberg, Keke (FIN)
Rosier, Louis (FRA)
Rosset, Ricardo (BRA)
Rothengatter, Huub (NED)
Salazar, Eliseo (CHI)
Salo, Mika (FIN)
Salvadori, Roy (GBR)
Sato, Takuma (JPN)
Scarfiotti, Lodovico (ITA)
Scheckter, Ian (RSA)
Scheckter, Jody (RSA)
Schell, Harry (USA)
Schlesser, Jean-Louis (FRA)
Schlesser, Jo (FRA)
Schneider, Bernd (GER)
Schumacher, Michael
  (GER)

Schumacher, Ralf (GER)
Seidel, Wolfgang (GER)
Senna, Ayrton (BRA)
Serafini, Dorino (ITA)
Servoz-Gavin, Johnny
  (FRA)
Siffert, Jo (SUI)
Speed, Scott (USA)
Stacey, Alan (GBR)
Stewart, Jackie (GBR)
Stewart, Jimmy (GBR)
Surtees, John (GBR)
Takagi, Tora (JPN)
Takahashi, Kunimitsu
  (JPN)
Tambay, Patrick (FRA)
Tarquini, Gabriele (ITA)
Taruffi, Piero (ITA)
Thackwell, Mike (NZL)
Trintignant, Maurice (FRA)
Trulli, Jarno (ITA)
Tuero, Estéban (ARG)
Van De Poele, Eric (BEL)
Vettel, Sébastien (GER)
Villeneuve, Gilles (CAN)
Villeneuve, Jacques
  (CAN)
Villeneuve, Jacques [Sr.]
  (CAN)
Villoresi, Luigi (ITA)
von Trips, Wolfgang
  (GER)
Warwick, Derek (GBR)
Watson, John (GBR)
Webber, Mark (AUS)
Wendlinger, Karl (AUT)
Wietzes, Eppie (CAN)
Williamson, Roger (GBR)
Wilson, Desiré (RSA)
Wurz, Alexander (AUT)
Zanardi, Alex (ITA)

✓ 72704

CITY BOYS

Don Gresswell Ltd., London, N.21   Cat. No. 1208   DG 02242/71